POLYMER CLAY
inspirations

PATRICIA KIMLE

NORTH LIGHT BOOKS
CINCINNATI, OH
www.artistsnetwork.com

acknowledgments

> "EVERY CHILD IS AN ARTIST. THE PROBLEM IS HOW TO REMAIN AN ARTIST ONCE HE GROWS UP."
> pablo. picasso

I live with three very creative children who show me every day in different ways how to remain an artist and live an artful life. To Jackson, who takes the scientific approach; to Nathan, who is the most freely expressive person I know; and to Erin, whose art is all about relationships—Mom loves you guys! The biggest thanks to my husband, Kevin, who has supported and believed in me and has never asked me to "get a real job."

Thanks also to my artistic sister, Colette. She has a fantastic visual imagination that we exercise by phone as she performs sounding board duties for me. No matter what I describe, I think she can see it in her mind's eye.

Every day, I praise my God for the gift of creativity and the chance to share it with others.

Thanks to Polyform Products, Inc. for generously providing all the clay used in the projects in this book. Also, thanks to Ellen Marshall and Jennifer Patterson for contributing projects to this book.

09 08 07 06 05   5 4 3 2 1

Library of Congress Cataloging-in-Publication Data
Kimle, Patricia
Polymer clay inspirations / Patricia Kimle.
  p. cm.
Includes index.
ISBN 1-58180-557-8 (pbk. : alk. paper)
  1. Polymer clay craft. I. Title.
TT297.K48 2004
738.1'2--dc22

Editor: Jennifer Fellinger
Cover Designer: Nick Gliebe, Design Matters
Interior Designer: Karla Baker
Layout Artist: Kathy Gardner
Production Coordinator: Robin Richie
Photographers: Patricia Kimle, Tim Grondin, Christine Polomsky

METRIC CONVERSION CHART

to convert	to	multiply by
Inches	Centimeters	2.54
Centimeters	Inches	0.4
Feet	Centimeters	30.5
Centimeters	Feet	0.03
Yards	Meters	0.9
Meters	Yards	1.1
Sq. Inches	Sq. Centimeters	6.45
Sq. Centimeters	Sq. Inches	0.16
Sq. Feet	Sq. Meters	0.09
Sq. Meters	Sq. Feet	10.8
Sq. Yards	Sq. Meters	0.8
Sq. Meters	Sq. Yards	1.2
Pounds	Kilograms	0.45
Kilograms	Pounds	2.2
Ounces	Grams	28.4
Grams	Ounces	0.04

about the author

Patricia Kimle has always been involved in art and design, from grade school on. Her early interests focused on clothing design, jewelry and wearable art. Patti holds a Ph.D. in Textiles and Clothing and taught Apparel Design at the college level for seven years. She has experience in many fields of art, including fashion drawing, fiber and textile design, and watercolor painting.

When her second child was born, Patti decided to stay at home and forge a new career as an artist working in polymer clay. For thirteen years, Patti has been exploring and designing with polymer clay. She teaches at workshops and conferences for art and polymer clay all over the country, including events such as the Bead & Button Show. She sells her polymer clay work in galleries and the occasional craft show.

Patti's work has appeared in many juried exhibitions for both open media and polymer clay. Her egg art has been selected to represent the state of Iowa at the White House Easter Egg display twice. Patti designs for magazines and her work has frequently appeared in publications for general crafts, jewelry and clay.

The mother of three creative children, an avid gardener and aspiring gourmet cook, Patti lives on a small "hobby" farm in Iowa with sheep and a duck. Although clay has crowded out most other art pursuits for the moment, she enjoys painting occasionally and is also a skilled knitter.

"MAY THE FAVOR OF THE LORD REST UPON US; ESTABLISH THE WORK OF OUR HANDS FOR US— YES, ESTABLISH THE WORK OF OUR HANDS."

psalm 90:17

These polymer clay pieces from 2003 feature my signature design. I adopted the design as the graphic logo for my business literature.

table of contents

PROJECTS INSPIRED BY nature 20

PROJECTS INSPIRED BY fabrics 48
and textiles

PROJECTS INSPIRED BY jewelry 70

PROJECTS INSPIRED BY fine art 94

INTRODUCTION

The word inspiration is derived from the Greek word for spirit. It means "the breath of life," or "the breath of God." Inspiration is what fills and animates our lives and our work. Inspiration is the spark, the force for action.

Since polymer clay is still a young medium, it is a field ripe with inspiration. Over the past decade, the exploratory, experimental attitude of polymer artists has yielded a vast array of styles and techniques for clay design. Art and craft materials and processes of all types have been incorporated into the growing body of polymer clay work. The question "What if?" inspires someone, which leads that individual to experiment, pursue answers and then report his or her results to a local guild or an e-mail list. The artist might then write an article and enter his or her work in a show or a gallery, and the news spreads. Questions inevitably follow: "Have you seen this? How did they do that?"

In my work with polymer clay, I have cultivated inspiration from many different sources. In some cases, my inspiration is a desire to imitate other materials. In others, it is a visual style or effect that I want to translate from another art form to my own polymer creation. No matter what drives me, I am always striving to develop new and innovative techniques. My aim is to share my own inspirations with you. This book is broken down into four sections, each featuring an inspirational theme for the polymer clay projects.

I live in the country, and I love nature and the changing seasons. Along with my kids, I also love rock collecting. So, the first section of this book features projects that were inspired by nature. There are many polymer clay techniques to imitate natural materials, including stones and leaves, and I have worked to develop new variations.

For years, I was involved in fiber art, fabric and fashion design. Though I rarely sew anymore, I still love fabrics, the source of inspiration for the second section in this book. A fabric sensibility—an awareness of pattern, motif and texture—relates very well to polymer clay work.

The third section, with projects inspired by jewelry, reflects a lifelong interest. As a kid, I was a costume jewelry nut. Today, I love fine art jewelry. Gold is my favorite metal, but I really haven't had an interest in learning metal work. So, I've been inspired to try nearly every gold paint and surface additive to find the most convincing substitute. You'll find the results of that quest in this section's set of projects.

I'm quite active in my local art center and have friends who are professional artists working in various media. After I took a watercolor class taught by a friend, I was inspired to find a way to paint on clay. The fourth and final section of this book contains projects inspired by other fine art forms, including watercolor.

I hope you enjoy making the projects in this book. Further, I hope you will be inspired to choose your own favorite medium of expression and ask yourself, "What if?"

materials and tools

A polymer clay artist, whether beginner or advanced, needs only a few basic supplies to produce successful results. In fact, some of the best clay artists don't use many tools beyond the basics. For some supplies, you don't have to look any farther than your own kitchen, sewing and craft stash. The tools that you may find can easily be adapted for polymer clay projects, while several materials can be combined with the clay itself.

POLYMER CLAY

Polymer clay is a synthetic modeling material that remains malleable until it is cured by baking at a low temperature. All polymer clays are basically made up of polyvinyl-chloride (PVC), pigment and solvents. During baking, the PVC granules melt and fuse and the solvents evaporate, leaving a durable product. Polymer clay can be used to make jewelry, home décor items, personal accessories and much, much more.

Polymer clay is available from several craft companies. The chemical composition for the brands vary, giving each slightly different working properties and finished characteristics. Brand preferences for polymer clay are a matter of personal choice. I recommend that beginners experiment with each brand to learn the *hand*, or feel, of the clay. In doing so, you'll discover how the clay responds while you are working with it and which techniques the clay is best suited for. By mixing clays of varying character, you can create a custom clay that is perfect for your working style.

SCULPEY III is a soft clay, easy to use straight from the package. Sculpey III is ideal for beginners and children as it doesn't require great hand strength. Rigid and somewhat brittle after baking, this clay is suitable for beads and home décor items that are fairly thick. Because of its brittle quality, Sculpey III is not recommended for thin pieces, protruding extensions or sculptures without an interior armature. Sculpey III comes in a wide range of colors, including pearls and metallics.

SCULPEY PREMO! is generally firmer than Sculpey III. Premo! is a strong clay that retains some flexibility after it is baked, especially in thin pieces. As my clay of choice, Premo! was used for all the projects in this book. Like Sculpey III, Premo! is available in many colors, including pearls and metallics.

Polymer clay
Clockwise from left: various brands of polymer clay, liquid clay, clay softener.

SCULPEY GRANITEX is clay mixed with colored fibers to simulate the look of stone, such as granite and rose quartz. Because the fibers in the clay tend to drag when the clay is cut by a blade, it is not good for slicing, caning or other techniques requiring clean cuts.

SCULPEY SUPERFLEX BAKE & BEND clay is extremely flexible after baking. It is ideal for using in kids' crafts and for making molds to use with additional polymer clay.

ORIGINAL SCULPEY is soft, white clay with a very chalky hand. It is quite brittle, but is good for interior filler and "bead guts."

SUPER SCULPEY is a flesh-colored clay that, when baked, is very hard with a translucent finish. It is a favorite for many doll sculptors.

FIMO CLASSIC is a very firm clay, much loved by artists who like to make intricate canes. Because Fimo can be dry or crumbly out of the package, it often requires more kneading before use. It is sometimes helpful to grind Fimo into a fine gravel consistency with a food processor, then work it into a smooth consistency by hand and with a pasta machine.

FIMOSOFT is a softer and more elastic clay, not as strong as Fimo but still somewhat flexible after baking. I find both Fimo and Fimosoft to have the driest hand of all the clays, which makes them a good choice for people with very warm hands. The FimoSoft line also features metallic and faux stone colors.

KATO POLYCLAY is quite strong and flexible after baking. It is a bit more rubbery than other clays and has a glossy sheen on the surface after baking. Kato Polyclay canes nicely and slices cleanly immediately after it has been reduced, unlike other brands that require a resting period before the clay can be sliced.

CERNIT clay is fairly firm out of the package but it is very responsive to warmth from handling. While it is being worked, the clay may become too soft, at which point it must rest to cool and firm up again before you continue working it. It is less flexible than some other clays but fairly strong. Cernit's appearance, which features a translucent sheen when baked, has been compared to porcelain. For this reason, doll makers also like Cernit clays.

LIQUID POLYMER CLAY is available under a number of brand names, including Liquid Sculpey, Kato Polyclay Clear Liquid Medium and Fimo Liquid Decorating Gel. Liquid clay may be used as a softener for solid clay and as a bonding aid when adding layers to previously baked parts. It may be tinted and used as paint, or it can be used as a transfer medium with print images. The clay's qualities, such as surface sheen, translucence and clarity, vary from formula to formula and brand to brand.

WORK SURFACES

Use a smooth, nonporous surface when working with polymer clay. A laminate countertop, a piece of Plexi-glass, or my favorite—a large glass cutting board—will all work, although they may become marked up by the cutting blades. Occasional sanding will restore the smooth surface. Do not put polymer on fine wood furniture as it may ruin the finish. Also useful are 6" (15cm) or 12" (30cm) ceramic tiles. A polymer clay piece may be created and baked on the tile to avoid moving and distorting the clay. Add a few extra minutes for baking time if you are baking on a tile surface, as tiles serve as insulators.

BASIC TOOLS

In addition to clay, there are several other materials and tools that you'll be working with. Most of the projects in this book require a pasta machine, an acrylic rod or brayer, clay blades, a craft knife and needle tools. However, you may find it helpful to review all the polymer clay supplies that are listed in the next few pages.

ROLLING TOOLS

Rolling polymer clay into smooth, even sheets is an essential first step in almost all techniques. Rolling, folding and rerolling sheets is also necessary for conditioning clay.

AN ACRYLIC ROD or brayer is the best tool for hand rolling sheets of clay; however, any smooth, lightweight tube will work as a rolling tool. I also find several sizes of thin brass tubing cut to a 6" (15cm) or 8" (20cm) length handy. If you roll your clay by hand, use a smooth item, such as a layer of cardboard on both sides of the clay to ensure an even sheet.

A PASTA MACHINE is invaluable for rolling smooth, even sheets of polymer clay at various thicknesses. Pasta machine motors by themselves are also available. Remember that pasta dough is much softer than polymer clay, so be reasonable in your expectations from the machine. Flatten a ball of clay to about ¼" (6mm) before passing it through the machine and never feed more than a double or triple folded sheet. Pasta machines rarely need to be cleaned, unless colors from one clay are showing up on the next. In this case, wipe the rollers with a dry paper towel. Do not immerse the machine in water or the parts may rust.

Rolling tools

Clockwise from right: pasta machine, brass rods, glass work surface over a ruled grid, acrylic rod

CUTTING TOOLS

Most projects require the cutting or slicing of measured strips, slabs, shapes and canes. A few simple cutting tools will make the job easy.

CLAY BLADES are usually about 6" (15cm) long and come in both flexible and rigid types.

A CRAFT KNIFE with replaceable blades is a must.

COOKIE CUTTERS, SHAPE TOOLS AND PUNCHES are available in all sorts of sizes, shapes and designs.

Texturing tools

Clockwise from top left: flexible mold, rubber stamps, sanding sponge, cornstarch powder, stair safety tread, clay strip mold, rubber stamp, clay leaf mold, resin flower and face molds, clay mold of button, plastic texturing sheets, two-part silicone compound and silicone molds of buttons

TIP

Never mix clay tools with food tools. If a tool comes from the kitchen, it should be dedicated to clay use and not used for food again.

Cutting tools

Clockwise from left: shape cutters, circle cutter set, flower cutters, decorative scissors, craft knife, clay blades, punches

TEXTURING TOOLS

Texture adds another dimension of design to polymer clay, offering unlimited possibilities for your clay projects. You can buy texturing tools or make and adapt your own.

MOLDS FOR FLOWERS, FIGURES, DECORATIVE ELEMENTS AND BODY PARTS are available in craft stores. Commercial molds are made from rigid resin, flexible rubber or clear plastic.

COMMERCIAL RUBBER STAMPS are also widely used with polymer clay. They can be found at craft, scrapbooking and rubber stamping supply stores.

PLASTIC TEXTURING SHEETS for etching or rubbing may also be used with clay. These can even be cut the same width as the pasta machine, then rolled through with the clay.

OBJECTS FOUND AROUND YOUR HOME can offer interesting textures or raised patterns. Textured designs on baskets, wood trim, glass, metal and ceramics can all be pressed into clay to create dimensional effects.

CLAY ITSELF may be used to make your own molds and texture plates by impressing the pattern or item into the clay, baking it, then using the clay mold in the same manner as a commercial mold. My favorite clay for making molds is Sculpey SuperFlex Bake & Bend.

SILICONE MOLD COMPOUNDS are useful for textures with extremely fine detail or items with small undercuts and interior spaces within the overall form. These compounds are two-part room temperature vulcanizing (RTV) formulas in which you mix equal portions of two putties until they are a consistent color. Press the molded item into the compound and let it set up for about 30 minutes. There are several brands available, some of which withstand temperatures far above the normal clay-curing temperature. Therefore, a molded design can be baked in the mold to avoid distortion that may otherwise occur while removing unbaked clay from a mold.

A MOLD RELEASE is necessary to keep the clay from sticking to most texture plates and molds. This can be any material that will prevent the clay from sticking too securely in the mold. Cornstarch powder can be dusted into the mold. Silicone automotive spray such as Armor All is also useful, although the silicone doesn't evaporate from the clay and may interfere with later surface embellishment. A fine mist of water will work with Sculpey clays because these clays resist water. Do not use water with Fimo or FimoSoft as it will increase the stickiness of the clay.

SCULPTING TOOLS

While this book does not include figurative sculpture projects, you'll still find a variety of sculpting tools quite useful. Sculpting tools produce texture and also help smooth and finish areas where our fingers are just too big or clumsy.

TOOLS MADE FOR CERAMICS AND POTTERY, such as sculpting tools, sgraffito needles and ball styluses can be adapted for use with polymer clay.

RUBBER-TIPPED CLAY SHAPERS are flexible, nonabsorbent tools that are a cross between a brush and a paint knife.

DENTAL TOOLS leave interesting impressions in clay (just don't think about what they used to do in someone's mouth!). Ask your dentist for any old tools.

SEWING, DARNING AND KNITTING NEEDLES are all excellent sculpting tools. Raid the sewing and needlework basket for various sizes. I have several sets of steel 0000 knitting needles that I use to pierce or hold beads.

DRILL BITS of various sizes can be embedded in clay handles. Turning the bits by hand is an easy way to make holes in baked beads and avoid distorting them when soft.

SPECIALIZED TOOLS

Hand rolling a set of uniformly sized and shaped beads is a challenge, and rolling thin, even strings of clay is nearly impossible to do by hand. Some specialized tools facilitate such tasks.

BEAD ROLLERS are cut plastic tubes that can slide against each other to smooth balls of clay inside. Available in many sizes, bead rollers come in round, oval and bicone shapes.

A CLAY EXTRUDER is a small barrel and plunger with a number of dies in various sizes and shapes. When extruding very small shapes or using stiff clay, this tool can be difficult to use. Add a little hand power to the extruder by adapting a caulking gun from the hardware store. An adapter disc to hold the clay extruder in place in the caulking gun is available from Poly-tools.com. Or, a large metal washer and a short piece of PVC plumbing pipe will also do the trick.

A CRAFT HEAT GUN can be used to set clay, including liquid clay, in a small area in order to proceed to the next step without waiting for a full baking cycle. Experiment with the heat gun and an oven thermometer to see how long it takes to bring an object to clay-baking temperatures.

Sculpting tools

Clockwise from bottom left: needle tools in clay handles, ball stylus, clay shapers, sculpting tools, orange stick, clay carving tools, dental tool, knitting needles, drill bits in clay handles

Specialized tools

Top to bottom: bead roller, heat gun, caulking gun, caulking gun adapter, clay extruder and dies

Useful additions

Clockwise from upper left: acrylic paints, oil paints, gold leaf, alcohol-based ink and marker, metallic paint pens, metal pulver, mica powder

USEFUL ADDITIONS

Polymer clay is compatible with a wide variety of art supplies, paints and pigment products. Many products can be applied directly onto the clay surface or kneaded and blended into clay.

DRY POWDERED PIGMENTS may be used to highlight the surface of unbaked clay. Chalks and pastels add color to clay, while metallic effects may be created with powdered mica such as Jacquard's Pearl-Ex powdered pigments or Lemon Tree…Etcetera's Powdered Pearls, and metal powders such as Eberhard Faber's metallic pulvers. Wear a dust mask when using powdered pigments and be careful not to disperse them into the air. When smoothed on with a brush or fingertip, these powders bond to the surface. Small amounts of loose powder may brush off after baking, but it is not always necessary to seal these with a varnish unless it is part of the design. The same powder products also may be mixed into light-color or translucent clay to tint it or create a pearlized sheen or a granular effect.

EMBOSSING POWDERS for rubber stamping are granules of thermoplastic resins. They melt at low temperatures and may be used on the surface of or blended into clay. Available in many colors, these powders are also quite useful in imitating the look of stone.

LEAFING PENS may be used to create a faux metal surface. I find Krylon leafing pens to be compatible with clay, and this brand comes in a range of colors, including gold, silver and copper. Always be cautious when using other leafing pens or metallic markers

because many are solvent-based and react with clay, softening it and making it gummy.

ANY WATER-BASED ACRYLIC PAINT is compatible with clay and may be used on the surface of soft or baked clay. However, some cheaper, low-quality paints may not adhere as well and consequently may chip off the surface. Lumiere metallic paints from Jacquard Products provide excellent coverage, even on black clay. Acrylic paint may be combined with soft clay if the paint is allowed to dry before it is folded or layered into the clay. If the acrylic doesn't dry first, the moisture creates steam as the clay is baked, resulting in bubbles or fissures.

OIL PAINT may be blended into soft clay as well. Unlike acrylic paint, however, oil paint may be incorporated into the clay immediately without waiting for it to dry first. Heat-set oil paints such as Genesis Artist Colors may be used on either soft or baked clay.

ALCOHOL-BASED INKS, such as Jacquard's Piñata Colors and Sanford's Prismacolor markers, may be used on soft or baked clay. Liquid inks are also useful for tinting liquid polymer clay. For stamping designs onto clay, try alcohol-based ink pads such as Brilliance by Tsukineko.

METAL LEAF is a great way to add the look of precious metal to clay designs without a high cost. Imitation (composition) metal leaf is available at craft stores in gold, silver, copper and variegated (oxidized copper). Real 23k gold and sterling silver are also available from higher end art stores and from jewelry suppliers. For silver, I recommend the imitation leaf, which is aluminum and will not tarnish the way sterling leaf will. I do, however, prefer the true color of 23k gold over composition gold. This real gold comes attached to sheets of tissue paper, making it easy to cut and handle efficiently. While the real gold may be a bit pricier, I've always found the results well worth the investment.

FINISHING SUPPLIES

Great finishing details will complement and enhance a good design. Using the right glue, sanding and buffing, and applying varnish are all aspects of achieving a superb finish.

GLUES

There are no perfect glues, and no glue is failure-proof. No one glue product works for every combination of clay, metal, paper and fiber. That said, I will make the following recommendations.

CYANOACRYLATE GLUE should be used to secure metal pieces, such as jewelry findings, to polymer clay. This includes most brands of instant or "crazy" glues. Select a medium- or slow-drying formula, which typically comes in the form of a thicker gel. Better brands are often found in the model-building section of hobby stores.

PVA WHITE GLUE (polyvinyl acetate adhesive) should be used to attach wood or paper to polymer clay. PVA glue, such as Sobo craft glue or Crafter's Pick Ultimate Glue, contains a vinyl component.

FABRIC GLUE, or glues made for attaching rhinestones to fabric, work well when attaching clay to fiber or fabric.

CONTACT CEMENT GLUES, such as E-6000 and Crafter's Goop, should be used for display pieces that will not be handled frequently or exposed to environmental changes. These glues deteriorate with time and lose their bonding power, a property that is accelerated with exposure to skin oils and friction. For this reason, I do not recommend contact cement for jewelry parts like pins and earring parts.

SANDING AND BUFFING MATERIALS

Use wet-dry sandpaper with water for polymer clay. The finer grits, numbered 320 and higher, are appropriate for polymer clay. Avoid sandpaper that is intended for wood as it is too coarse for clay. Wet-dry sandpaper is usually black or gray and is available in hardware stores up to 800-grit. If you want to progress through even finer grits, 1000-, 1500- and 2000-grit may be found in the automotive

section of most discount department stores. Wet-dry sanding surfaces are also available in 1/4" (6mm) foam sheets and sponge blocks. These are easy to hold and cause less strain on the hand muscles; however, I find the sponge types wear out more quickly and thus are more expensive. My solution is to cut sandpaper into strips and wrap it around an old block.

Buffing or polishing may be done by hand with a soft cloth or a rotary tool. A rotary hand tool can be fitted with a 1" (2.5cm) diameter muslin disc. A jeweler's lathe or a bench grinder can accommodate much larger muslin wheels and will polish larger surfaces more quickly. The wheels should be cotton muslin and unstitched. Lathes and muslin are available from a jeweler's supplier. A bench grinder from the hardware store can be adapted by removing all guard pieces around the wheel and substituting the muslin disc for the stone grinding wheel.

FINISHES AND VARNISHES

There are many liquid varnish and gloss products that work with clay and others that do not. Use only water-based products with clay. Sculpey and Fimo both make safe finishes. Many artists use acrylic floor wax or water-based wood varnish. Oil-based varnishes contain solvents that will react with clay over time and soften the surface, making it tacky and gummy. Aerosol finishes are generally not compatible with clay. Some contain solvents, while others contain hydrocarbon propellents that react with clay.

Sanding and buffing materials

Left to right: sandpapers, rotary tool, jeweler's lathe with muslin buffing wheel

Finishes

Various water-based finishes that I have found to be compatible with polymer clay

techniques

The variety of polymer clay techniques has expanded rapidly in the last decade as the medium has grown in popularity. Many of the projects in this book require you to create Skinner blends, canes and metallic effects. These popular techniques, as well as basic handling, baking and finishing techniques, are covered in the following pages.

CONDITIONING THE CLAY

When polymer clay is taken out of the package, it first must be *conditioned* to create a more workable consistency. To condition polymer clay, roll or knead the clay until a smooth, consistent sheet can be made from it. The required amount of conditioning varies according to the brand, age and consistency of the clay.

Occasionally, very dry or crumbly clay may need to be softened to make it smooth. Sculpey Clay Softener (formerly labeled Diluent) is an oil solvent sold for this purpose. A few drops of mineral oil also will work.

On the other hand, clay straight from the package may be too soft for some techniques. This can be remedied by **leaching** the clay. To do this, press sheets of clay between clean absorbent paper, such as printer/copier paper or blank newsprint. The paper will absorb excess oil from the clay. You can leach the clay for a few hours or a day or so, depending on how soft the clay is and how firm the desired result.

CREATING A SKINNER BLEND

The Skinner blend is named for Judith Skinner, the artist who developed an easy technique to blend colors into smooth gradations. The basic blend is made with two color sheets cut into right triangles. More complex blends can be made with multiple colors arranged across a sheet. Using the gradations of blended colors as the basis for cane building allows for extraordinary color pattern effects.

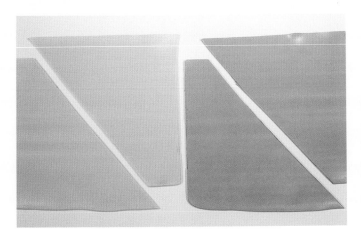

1 roll and cut sheet

Using the thickest setting on the pasta machine, roll each color into a sheet the full width of the machine. Cut each sheet in half diagonally.

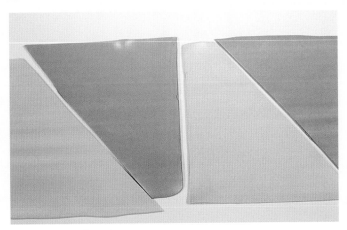

2 arrange clay pieces

Arrange the four pieces into two square sheets, each composed of two different-colored triangular pieces.

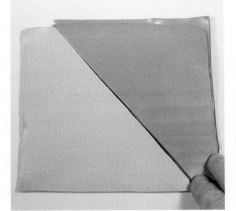

3 stack and roll clay

Stack the pieces by placing one set of triangles on top of the other, maintaining the square shape and keeping the colors uniform on each side. Roll this stack through the pasta machine with the solid color edges to the right and left.

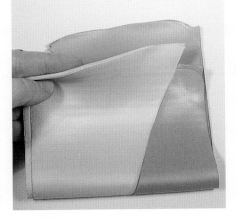

4 fold sheet

Fold the sheet in half from bottom to top.

5 roll clay until blended

Run the folded sheet through the pasta machine, feeding the folded edge first. Repeat steps 4 and 5 until the sheets are thoroughly blended, with a gradation of color and no hard lines showing.

MAKING AND REDUCING CANES

A cane is a log or loaf of clay with a pattern of various colors running through its length. Slicing across the cane reveals a cross section of the design. All slices should be identical throughout the cane's length. Canework is often called *millefiore* (Italian for *many flowers*), which refers to a specific type of glass crafting.

Canes may be round, square or irregularly shaped, and the basis of their designs may be simple geometric shapes, repeated patterns or pictorial images. The appealing aspect of canes is that the sides of a log or loaf may be compressed, but the arrangement of color and pattern remains intact as the cane is reduced.

TIP

Distortion typically occurs in the reduction process, leading to some waste at the ends of the log or loaf. You'll notice distortion if you try to create a log by rolling the clay back and forth across a surface like a snake or when you roll a loaf with a rod. Rolling applies the most pressure and warmth to the outside layers of clay, so the outside tends to move faster than the center of the cane, creating distortion.

In theory, a 1" (2.5cm) cube can be reduced to ½" x ½" x 4" (13mm x 13mm x 10cm). It can then be cut into four 1" (2.5cm) pieces and reassembled into a 1" (2.5cm) cube. This formula is useful when planning the amount of clay needed for a project. Depending on the firmness of the clay, I find a 15–20 percent allowance for distortion and waste to be a good estimate.

1 roll clay log

Roll a 2" × ½" (5cm × 13cm) log of one color. Wrap a sheet of clay around the log and trim the ends evenly.

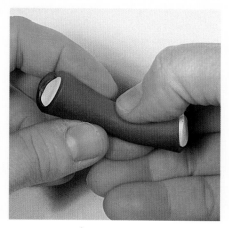

2 squeeze from center out

To avoid distortion when reducing a cane, use squeezing force on the cane, working from the center toward each end. For a log, create a "dog bone" and work pressure outward until the diameter is equal along the length. For a loaf, squeeze from the center along two opposite sides, then rotate and squeeze the other two sides.

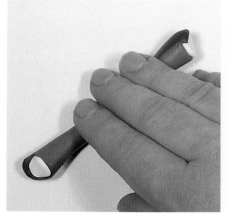

3 roll cane to restore shape

Lay the cane on the work surface. To restore the circular shape, use your fingers to gently roll the cane across the surface. To restore square corners, roll an acrylic rod across each side.

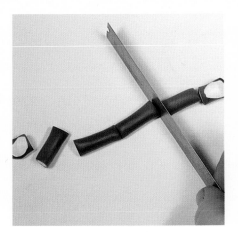

4 cut off distorted ends

With a clay blade, cut the distorted portion off the ends and cut the cane into four equal pieces.

5 assemble pieces

Assemble the cut pieces into a cluster, with their lengths running parallel, to form a desired pattern. Compress the sides, working from the center outward.

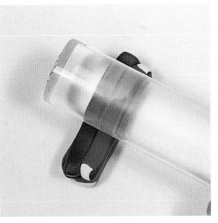

6 roll clay into square

Roll the clay with an acrylic rod to shape the cluster into a square. Cut into four equal pieces and reassemble into a square. Reduce to desired size.

TIP

I like to make cane patterns into sheets like fabric and use the sheets to cover or "upholster" larger forms.

7 slice cane

Slice off the distorted ends. The finished cane may be sliced for various purposes. Thick slices may be pierced to make flat beads and thin slices may be rolled onto a ball of clay for a round bead. Slices may also be applied to another surface or form.

Cut slices as thin and as uniform as possible. Roll the distorted end waste into a backing sheet, then lay out the slices side by side on top of the sheet.

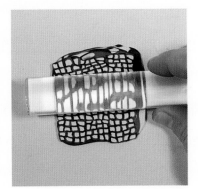

Use an acrylic rod to roll the seams together and consolidate the sheet. If you intend to roll the clay through the pasta machine again, remember that the pattern will grow a little larger. Plan for this by overreducing the cane to a slightly smaller scale.

BAKING

Most polymer clays are cured between 265° and 285°F (129°–140°C) and should be baked for 30 minutes per ¼" (6mm) thickness. Manufacturers' recommendations vary slightly from brand to brand, so check the label of the package you are using.

Clay may be baked in a home oven or in a countertop oven, such as a toaster or convection oven. Always use an oven thermometer when baking clay to make sure the temperature is accurate. If clay isn't baked hot enough for long enough, the PVC granules may not completely fuse and the finished product will be brittle and prone to damage. If the clay exceeds the curing temperature, it can begin to darken in color, scorch and even burn. Burning clay will produce toxic fumes.

If you do not like the normal baking odor, you can ventilate the room. If your climate permits, place your oven outdoors or in a garage. Avoid drafts, however, as this may interfere with the oven's ability to maintain a consistent temperature.

NOTE

Baking clay normally has a slight odor that is harmless. However, if you see smoke or smell a very acrid odor, turn the oven off, remove the clay from the oven and ventilate the room immediately.

SANDING

To improve the overall quality of a polymer clay design, it is important to finish the piece with a thorough sanding. Use wet-dry sandpaper to sand the clay surface, keeping the sandpaper wet and rinsing the paper often. Polymer clay should not be sanded dry, as the dust is both messy and hazardous to inhale.

When you sand a surface, begin with coarser grit and progress to finer grit. Most objects can start with 400-grit sandpaper or extra-fine sanding sponges. If the project is rough or has a lot of imperfections, 320- or even 220-grit will cut the surface quickly. However, these coarse grits will leave some scratches that must be sanded out with higher grits. If a surface will be finished with an acrylic glaze product, a 600-grit sanding should be adequate. For buffing with a muslin wheel, higher grits such as 800 and 1000 may be desired.

By creating the smoothest possible surface before baking, you will make all sanding jobs easier. I also find that the job goes faster if you sand a clay piece while it is still warm from the oven. You can add a few drops of dish soap or rinse aid to the water to keep the sandpaper from clogging up.

BUFFING OR VARNISHING

For a nice shine, buff your polymer clay piece at high speed with a jeweler's lathe, a bench grinder or a rotary tool that has been fitted with a muslin wheel. To get a soft sheen instead of a high shine, buff the clay surface by hand for a minute or so with a piece of worn denim. You can also apply liquid varnish or gloss products to give your clay piece a finishing touch. See page 13 for a discussion of finishing products.

Practice good safety habits when working with power tools, such as lathes or grinders. Do not wear loose clothing or hanging straps. Tie long hair back out of the way. Buff beads individually before stringing them. Keep the clay object in the lower-front quadrant of the spinning muslin wheel. The wheel tends to grab items away and send them ricocheting around the room, so place a soft item a few feet behind the wheel to catch them. A buffing mantra I learned from a friend is: "Hold tightly and press lightly."

CREATING METALLIC EFFECTS

Premo! Sculpey, Kato Polyclay and FimoSoft all offer metallic and/or pearl colors. To create this distinctive metallic and pearl look, mica powder is incorporated into the clay. If you've ever found mica in its natural state, you've probably noticed that it forms in sheets. Even ground-up mica maintains a flakelike particle. When these specialty clays are conditioned into sheets, the mica particles become aligned parallel to the direction of the sheet and create a grain. Tone-on-tone designs can be made from a single color clay by creating and then manipulating the grain of the mica in the sheet. You can achieve many subtle effects with metallic and pearl clay, including *invisible caning* and *ghost images* (see images at right).

You may notice that metallic and pearl clay straight from the package appears darker across the cut surface. This is because the mica particles in unconditioned clay lie in all different directions. When the clay is conditioned, the color appears bright and even because the mica particles, now parallel with the surface, reflect light from the surface uniformly.

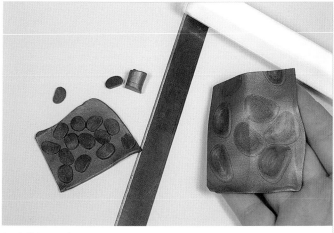

Invisible caning

To create the effect of invisible caning, condition a sheet of metallic or pearl clay, then roll it into a spiral cane. Lay slices of the cane on top of a sheet of the same clay, then roll the sheet until the slices are smooth on the surface. The grain follows the spiral like an old vinyl record album, and the slices reflect light in various directions to create a visual pattern on the clay's perfectly smooth surface.

Ghost image

This is an example of a ghost image. To achieve this effect, use a rubber stamp to impress a design into a sheet of conditioned metallic or pearl clay. Hold a clay blade almost parallel to the surface, then shave off the raised areas. The surface is smooth, but the design image remains.

COVERING EXISTING FORMS

Polymer's low curing temperature provides a great deal of freedom for mixing mediums in your artwork. Anything that can withstand 285°F (140°C) can be combined with clay, including wood, paper, metal, glass and some plastics. To cover a glass or metal form, simply roll the clay into sheets and wrap it around the form, taking care to press all air bubbles out.

Interior forms can be permanent or temporary. I often use interesting glass shapes to form a base layer of black or gray clay. After baking, I cut the clay off the glass, holding my craft knife at an angle to the surface. Then I reassemble the clay pieces using cyanoacrylate glue and add the design layer on top.

Clay does not stick well to more porous surfaces such as cardboard, wood or papier mâché. Before covering these items with clay, the surface must first be coated with a smooth sealant to which the clay can adhere. Two coats of white glue work well for paper and cardboard, and water-based varnish works for wood.

NOTE

Test all plastics in the oven for a few minutes before putting time and effort into a design that could be ruined. Never use Styrofoam with polymer clay as most types of Styrofoam release toxic fumes when heated.

STORING POLYMER CLAY

Because polymer clay does not contain water, it does not dry out as earthen clay does. Over time, however, it will become firmer and drier and it will gather dust. Clay that is out of its original packaging can be stored wrapped in plastic bags or foil. Clay should not be stored unwrapped in rigid, clear acrylic boxes or drawers because the solvents in the clay will bond with the box and both the container and the clay will be ruined.

PROJECTS INSPIRED BY *nature*

Nature is a never-ending source of ideas. This is evident in the first set of projects, all of which are inspired by the natural world. With these projects, you'll be imitating some of nature's most beautiful treasures, such as leaf fossils, mother-of-pearl, turquoise and granite. Before you begin working on each project, consider the object that serves as the source, noting its scale, shape, color, surface patterns and textures. Many of the sources that I have selected are small in scale with an organic shape, subtle color contrasts and granular or striated patterns. Several have richly textured natural surfaces, some with a characteristic patina.

Various types of paints and powders are useful in giving your polymer clay object the look of these distinctive surfaces. Many precious natural materials also have a highly polished surface, so excellent sanding and finishing will give your piece a final, convincing touch.

turquoise
bracelet and ring

In this project, I use embossing powders and small amounts of colored clay to simulate the look of the *matrix*, the variety of minerals and other materials embedded in the turquoise stone. To create the linear quality of the matrix, I use metallic gold paint. However, silver, Burnt Umber or Quinacridone Gold paint all will achieve the same convincing effect. Feel free to alter the recipe to vary the shade of turquoise, and do not hesitate to add as few or as many matrix materials as you wish. Buffing rather than varnishing will result in a finish that more closely imitates the sheen of real stone.

materials and tools

- 2 oz. (57g) turquoise clay
- marble-sized ball plus one pea-sized ball of black clay
- marble-sized ball of gold clay
- marble-sized ball of translucent clay
- pea-sized ball of medium blue clay
- liquid acrylic paint: metallic gold
- ½ teaspoon (4g) black embossing powder
- ½ teaspoon (4g) gold embossing powder
- ½ teaspoon (4g) white embossing powder
- sterling silver channel ring
- sterling silver cuff bracelet with raised edges
- acrylic rod or brayer
- cheese grater with coarse and fine shredders
- clay blade
- fingernail buffing board
- jeweler's lathe with muslin wheel
- palette knife
- pasta machine
- wet-dry sandpaper, 400- and 600-grit
- waxed paper

INSPIRATION: TURQUOISE

When you examine real turquoise, you see that there are slight variations in color, ranging from light green to very blue. The most valuable stones contain large, pure chunks of turquoise, with little or no matrix. The matrix consists of minerals and other materials, often gray or brown, embedded in the stone.

1 prepare clay

Divide the turquoise clay into three equal portions. Set one portion of pure turquoise aside for step 7. Condition and set another portion of pure turquoise aside, pictured at left, for the next step. Mix the black and blue pea-sized balls of clay into the remaining portion to create a slightly darker shade of turquoise, pictured at right, for the next step.

2 shred clay

Against the coarse shredder of a cheese grater, grate two portions of the turquoise clay—the pure turquoise and the darker shade—into a pile on a sheet of waxed paper. Against the fine shredder, grate the gold, translucent and remaining black clay into the same pile.

3 mix clay bits

Gently toss the shredded bits together to mix the clay. Sprinkle the embossing powders over the pile.

4 add paint to mixture

Use a palette knife to spread gold paint over the pile, then stir the mix together with the knife. Start with about one teaspoon of paint and add more as necessary, up to one tablespoon, until the paint covers all the bits of clay. Let the pile sit for several minutes until the paint is mostly dry but still slightly tacky.

5 compress clay

Gather the mass of shredded clay and firmly compress it into a 1" (2.5cm) square log, approximately 4" (10cm) in length. The paint decreases the stickiness of the clay, so the process of compressing the clay may take some time. Continue to compress the clay until it doesn't break up or crack as you press on it.

6 slice lengthwise pieces

Using a clay blade, slice ⅛" (3mm) thick slices lengthwise from the log.

7 consolidate clay into sheet

Roll out the reserved portion of turquoise clay to a sheet ⅟₁₆" (1.5mm) thick. Lay the log slices in a row on top of the sheet, then roll with the acrylic rod to consolidate the slices into the sheet and blend the seams. Roll the clay through the pasta machine until it is thin enough to fill the bracelet and ring channels, approximately ⅟₁₆" (1.5mm).

8 apply clay to bracelet and ring

Cut a strip of clay the length and width of the bracelet channel, then press the clay firmly into the channel. Trim it to fit. Gently smooth the clay to remove any fingerprints. Repeat for the ring channel. Trim the ends of the clay to meet flush, then blend the seam. Bake the bracelet and the ring. Cool.

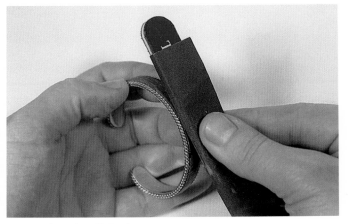

9 sand and polish clay

Wrap the 400-grit wet-dry sandpaper around a fingernail buffing board to sand the clay without damaging the silver edges of the pieces. Repeat with the 600-grit sandpaper. Polish the clay with a muslin wheel on a jeweler's lathe.

To achieve a beautiful finished product that will withstand the test of time, remember this: the presence of acrylic paint in the matrix weakens the bonds of the polymer clay. The paint lines can become fault lines where a piece could crack or chip. To compensate, any pieces made with the addition of acrylic paint need to use a backing sheet, an armature, or have liquid clay mixed into the matrix or brushed over the surface. In this project, a backing sheet was used.

granite
bead choker necklace

The granules in granite, a mixture of quartz, feldspar and other minerals, give the stone its distinct look. These granular shapes are relatively small in scale, so try to create little shavings from the clay—not big chunks or strings—for the right effect. Black and gold embossing powder creates the natural look of impurities within the clay "stone." As with the turquoise project, this recipe uses paint to fashion a matrix between the chunks of clay. The paint also provides color, so feel free to use any color of metallic paint you wish.

materials and tools

- 1 oz. (28g) pearl clay
- 1 oz. (28g) translucent clay
- ½ oz. (14g) gold metallic clay
- marble-sized ball of silver metallic clay
- pea-sized ball of black clay
- pea-sized ball of gold metallic clay
- liquid polymer clay
- liquid acrylic paint: blue
- metallic liquid acrylic paint: silver or pewter
- ½ teaspoon (4g) black embossing powder
- ½ teaspoon (4g) gold embossing powder
- beading wire, approximately 30" (76cm) long
- hard brass wire, 1/32" (1mm) diameter, two 12" (30cm) lengths
- barrel clasp
- crimp beads
- 3mm hematite beads
- cheese grater with coarse and fine shredders
- clay blade
- crimping pliers
- palette knife
- wet-dry sandpaper, 320-, 400- and 600-grit
- waxed paper

INSPIRATION: GRANITE

Little boys like collecting rocks—at least mine do. My impulse to make convincing rocks was largely inspired by my oldest son. One of his favorite rocks is granite, which features a little sparkle and some color variation in the granules. The idea was conceived after listening to rocks go 'round and 'round the dryer (after falling out of his jeans pockets) for the zillionth time!

27

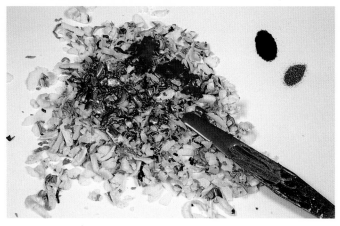

1 prepare clay

Using the coarse shredder of a cheese grater, grate the pearl and translucent clays into a pile on a sheet of waxed paper. Use the fine shredder to grate the silver, black and gold clays into the same pile. Gently toss the shredded bits together to mix the colors. Sprinkle the embossing powders over the pile. With a palette knife, spread blue and silver paint over the pile. Start with about one teaspoon of each color and add more as necessary.

2 combine mixture

With a palette knife, stir the mixture together until all the bits of clay are coated with paint. Let the pile sit for several minutes until the paint is mostly dry but still slightly tacky.

3 insert wire into logs

Compress the shredded clay to form a log, approximately ¾" (2cm) in diameter and 8" (20cm) long. Divide the log into two lengths, then lay both on a sheet of waxed paper. Insert a piece of brass wire into the end of one log, passing it through the length of the clay until it comes out the other end. Repeat with the other log, using another brass wire.

4 bake logs

Compress and consolidate the clay on the wire by alternately pinching and rolling until each log is approximately ⅜" (9mm) in diameter. Apply a liberal coat of liquid clay to the surface of each log. Squeeze the liquid into all the cracks and crevices, then smooth it in with your fingers to ensure the clay has adequate bonding. Bake. Cool. Remove wires.

5 slice clay

Wet-sand the clay logs, beginning with 320-grit sandpaper and progressing through to 400- and 600-grit. It is easier to slice baked clay if it is warm, so return the sanded logs to the oven for a few minutes. When warm, use a clay blade to slice the clay into ⅜" (9mm) lengths.

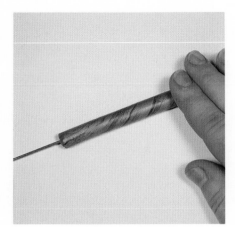

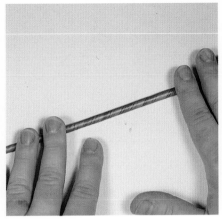

6 insert wire into gold log

Use your hands to shape the gold metallic clay into a log. Insert a piece of brass wire into one end of the log, passing it through the length of the clay until it comes out the other end.

7 elongate gold log and bake

Elongate the log by rolling the clay on the wire back and forth. Twist the clay around the wire frequently while rolling to keep it centered. Roll the log to ¼" (6mm) diameter, then bake.

8 slice clay

After the clay has cooled enough to handle, remove the wire. Slice the log into ¹⁄₁₆" (1.5mm) thick donut beads.

9 string necklace

Thread a crimp bead onto the length of beading wire, then thread the wire through the loop of a barrel clasp. Next, thread 2" (5cm) of the wire end back through the crimp bead and squeeze the crimp closed. Add the first several hematite beads onto the wire, over the tail, then trim the tail. Continue to add the hematite and clay beads in an alternating pattern until you reach the desired length. Finish the other end with a second crimp bead in the same manner.

This recipe makes enough beads for a matching bracelet. To create a bracelet, string the beads as you did for the necklace, using a shorter length of wire. Magnet clasps are wonderful for bracelets.

leaf fossil
pendant and box

Dirt, moss, decay, moisture, abrasion—all are evident on a piece of old wood, creating a natural surface patina that bespeaks the

passing of time. Under the aged patina remain the grain and pattern from the life of the tree. To make this leaf fossil pendant,

start with the tree itself. Take a walk outside and collect a few leaves with striking shapes and designs. Choose one of these

leaves for your mold, which you'll then use to create the pendant. You can "fossilize" the pendant by adding a faux patina with

various acrylic paints. If you really want authenticity, you can rub on a little dirt or earthen clay!

materials and tools

- 2 oz. (57g) ecru or beige clay
- pea-sized ball of brown clay
- 1 oz. (28g) Sculpey SuperFlex Bake & Blend clay, any color
- liquid polymer clay
- liquid acrylic paints: Burnt Umber and Verdigris
- metallic liquid acrylic paint (optional)
- papier mâché hinged box, approximately 2¾" × 3¼" × 4¾" (7cm × 8cm × 12cm)
- 3mm black rubber cord, desired length for pendant
- 18-gauge gold wire, 4" (10cm) long

- barrel clasp
- end caps
- fabric for lining box (optional)
- leaf or cluster of foliage
- small twig
- cyanoacrylate glue
- PVA white glue
- cornstarch powder
- acrylic rod or brayer
- burnishing tool
- clay blade
- clay modeling tools: clay shapers, knife, stiff brush

- craft knife
- glass sheet (optional)
- hand drill with ¹⁄₃₂" (13mm) bit
- ½" (13mm) flat paintbrushes
- pasta machine
- round-nose pliers
- screwdriver
- texturing tools: coarse sandpaper or safety tread
- V-shaped carving tool
- wire cutter
- container for diluted glue
- paper towels

INSPIRATION: LEAVES

With its symmetry and simplicity, a single leaf exemplifies the perfect design work of Mother Nature. Sometimes in nature, the most beautiful things stick around for a while. Leaves can be preserved for millions of years in fossilized form. Fortunately, with polymer clay, you don't have to wait quite so long to create your own fossilized leaf!

1 roll out sheet

Roll the SuperFlex clay into a sheet about half the thickness of your thickest pasta machine setting (see *Tip*, at right). Sprinkle cornstarch powder over the sheet and, with your hands, rub it across the surface to eliminate all tackiness from the clay.

TIP

All pasta machines vary slightly, so for this project, thickness measurements will be specific to the pasta machine you are using. You will need to experiment a bit to determine your specifications. The mold sheet should be just over half the thickness of the thickest pasta machine setting. (On my 7-step Atlas pasta machine, for which setting 1 is the thickest, the appropriate setting is a 4.) To test the thickness, roll a sheet of clay to what you think is about the half your machine's ultimate thickness and fold it in half. Run the clay through the machine at its thickest setting. The sheet should not get very much longer (no more than about 10 percent of the folded length), but if it doesn't elongate at all, then you have made the sheet too thin.

2 create leaf mold

Center the leaf on the powdered side of the clay sheet, then carefully roll the sheet with the leaf through the pasta machine at the same setting used in the previous step. After removing the clay from the pasta machine, peel the leaf off and lay the sheet out flat.

3 repair tears

If the stem of the leaf made a tear in clay, lay the clay on a sheet of glass, impression side up. Lift up the sheet just enough to spread a bit of liquid clay on the glass where the torn area will touch. Press the sheet down. Using a fine paintbrush, wipe any excess liquid clay that seeps through to the top. Bake on the glass at 285°F (140°C). Cool.

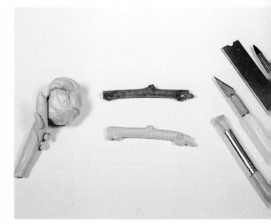

4 create twig

While the mold is baking, shape the clay twig from which the fossil pendant will hang. Use a knife, modeling tool, stiff brush or any other tools to shape and texture the clay to your satisfaction. It may help to select a real twig for inspiration. Bake. Cool.

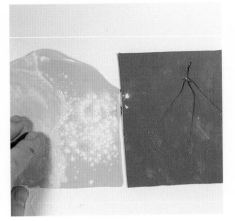

5 create interior form for pendant

Roll out the ecru clay to a sheet approximately ⅛" (3mm) thick. With a clay blade, cut the sheet to the shape you want your pendant to be. Pinch around the edges to bevel them slightly. Bake. Cool.

6 create sheet for front pendant piece

Roll out the leftover ecru clay into a sheet the same thickness as your mold and about the same size. Powder the sheet with cornstarch to eliminate all tackiness. Place the powdered side of the sheet against the textured side of the mold and run through the pasta machine on its thickest setting.

7 remove sheet from mold

Carefully peel the mold from the ecru sheet.

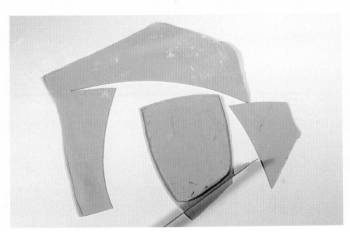

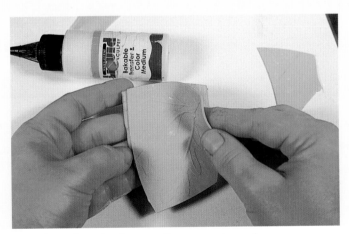

8 cut front pendant piece

Cut the front pendant piece from the molded ecru sheet, using the interior form you created in step 5 as a pattern. The leaf impression will provide the design on the pendant, so before you cut, consider what part of the impression you want to appear on the pendant shape and then crop the impression accordingly.

9 adhere interior form to front pendant piece

Match up the interior form with the pendant piece so that the edges meet and the leaf impression faces out. Separate the two pieces and apply a thin layer of liquid clay to the interior form. Gently press the pendant piece and the interior form together.

10 create back pendant piece

Create the back pendant piece by repeating steps 6–9 with the last of the ecru clay. Once all three pieces have been adhered together with liquid clay, press the edges together slightly, leaving a ³⁄₃₂" (2mm) gap around the top and bottom edges. Trim any excess clay. Bake. Cool.

11 seal edges and bake

Roll the brown clay into a thin snakelike form. Press the brown clay into the gap around the edges of the pendant, then texture the clay with sandpaper or tread. Trim any excess clay. Bake the pendant. Cool.

12 paint clay

Using a paintbrush, apply a coat of Burnt Umber acrylic paint to the surface of the twig and both sides of the pendant.

13 wipe paint from surface

Allow the paint to dry for two or three minutes only. With a damp paper towel, rub off some of the paint. Repeat with Verdigris acrylic paint.

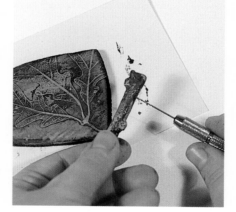

14 drill holes

With a hand drill, make two holes through the clay twig, placing the holes about ¹⁄₂" (13mm) from each end. Drill two holes into the top edge of the pendant, placing the holes the same distance apart as the holes in the twig.

TIP

When making lidded forms, don't cut across the vessel opening until after baking; the lid will fit better and the pattern will match up perfectly. However, if the vessel is sealed airtight by the clay, it will need a tiny hole somewhere so that expanding air can escape during baking.

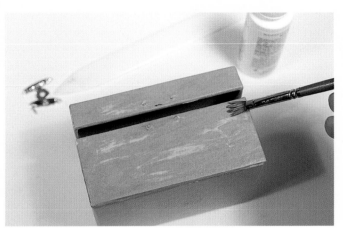

15 assemble necklace

Cut the gold wire into two 2" (5cm) lengths. With round-nose pliers, make a hangman's loop on one end of each wire. Push the opposite end of the wires through the holes in the twig and into the corresponding pendant holes. Secure the wire in the pendant holes with a drop of cyanoacrylate glue. String the cord through the wire loops, adjusting it to the desired length for a necklace. Glue end caps onto the cord and attach a clasp. Or glue the spliced cord together for a necklace long enough to fit over one's head.

16 cover box with clay and bake

With pliers or a screwdriver, remove the lock from the front of the papier mâché box. Smooth the holes with a burnishing tool. Seal the papier mâché surface by painting the box with a thin layer of diluted white glue, then allow the glue to dry. Create clay sheets with leaf impressions, as you did in steps 6–7, then use the sheets to cover the box on all sides, pressing the clay firmly onto the box. You may need additional smooth sheets of clay to fill any voids. Smooth all the seams. Do not cut across the vessel opening (see *Tip*, page 34). Bake.

17 finish box

While the clay is still warm, use a craft knife to cut through the front and side edges of the box lid. With a V-shaped carving tool, carve along the back hinge line. Paint the surface of the box with the Burnt Umber and Verdigris paints as with the pendant, using a damp paper towel to remove some of the paint after it has nearly dried.

You can embellish the inside of the box by painting it with a metallic acrylic paint or by lining it with fabric.

checkerboard set

This checkerboard set is divided into two projects: the checkerboard and the checkers. The set's elements imitate beautiful materials from nature—mother-of-pearl, paua shell, jade and malachite. In both projects, ink, acrylic paint and embossing powders are used to capture the unique qualities of these materials. When you're finished, you'll have a masterpiece that looks like an aged heirloom.

materials and tools

FOR CHECKERBOARD:
- 5 oz. (142g) pearl clay, divided into one 3 oz. (85g) piece and one 2 oz. (57g) piece
- 1 oz. (28g) translucent clay, divided into two ½ oz. (14g) pieces
- ½ oz. (14g) black clay
- liquid acrylic paints: black and Burnt Umber
- Piñata inks: Baja Blue, Burro Brown, Havana Brown, Lime Green, Passion Purple, Sapphire Blue, Señorita Magenta, Shadow Grey and Sunbright Yellow
- 70% isopropyl (rubbing) alcohol
- wooden cigar box with sliding top, approximately 6¾" × 8½" × 1½" (17cm × 22cm × 4 cm)
- PVA white craft glue
- water-based varnish
- wet-dry sandpaper, 400- and 600-grit

FOR CHECKERS:
- 1 oz. (28g) green clay
- ¾ oz (21g) translucent clay
- ½ oz. (14g) plus one marble-sized ball of turquoise clay
- marble-sized ball of black clay
- marble-sized ball of red clay
- liquid acrylic paints: Quinacridone Gold and Verdigris
- metallic acrylic paint: gold
- Piñata inks: Rainforest Green and Mantilla Black
- ¼ teaspoon (2g) black embossing powder
- ¼ teaspoon (2g) Verdigris embossing powder
- two-part silicone molding compound
- circle die cutter, ½" (13mm) diameter
- button with a raised geometric pattern, ½" (13mm) diameter
- button with a raised heraldic pattern, ½" (13mm) diameter

FOR BOTH:
- acrylic rod or brayer
- clay blade
- craft knife
- metal ruler
- ¼" (6mm) flat and medium round paintbrushes
- pasta machine
- right angle
- disposable cups
- paper towels

INSPIRATION: MOTHER-OF-PEARL AND PAUA SHELL

Pictured here is mother-of-pearl inside a paua shell, just two of the inspirations for these projects. Mother-of-pearl is formed within mollusk shells as the creature releases protective secretions throughout its lifetime. Subtle and luminous layers of color result. I like to imagine that the varying colors are a record of the creature's life challenges and achievements—and I find a lesson in the fact that more variety is more highly prized!

CHECKERBOARD

The checkerboard will be composed of faux mother-of-pearl and faux paua shell. In nature, these two materials have a beautiful patina and pearlescence, so, to imitate their appearance, pearl clay will be used. In addition, the color pattern of both mother-of-pearl and paua shell is more smoothly striated than it is granular, so you'll be working with clay sheets rather than crumbles.

TIP

When you are staining a small wooden object, acrylic paints are a very economical alternative to wood stain. Instead of buying an entire can of stain, you can mix only the amount of paint needed. In addition, acrylic paint dries quickly and is easy to clean up.

1 paint box

Mix one part Burnt Umber and one part black acrylic paint, then dilute with water to make a thin consistency, similar to commercial wood stain. Paint the wooden box inside and out with this mixture. Wipe off any excess paint with a paper towel. Let dry. Apply two coats of varnish to the interior and one coat to the exterior. Let dry.

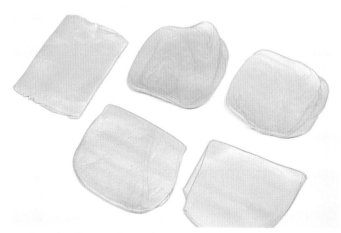

2 tint clay for mother-of-pearl sheet

Divide 3 oz. (85g) pearl clay into six flat pieces. Set one piece aside for step 9. With the round brush, paint the surface of one piece with Havana Brown ink, another with Baja Blue, another with Señorita Magenta, and another with Sunbright Yellow (clean the brush with rubbing alcohol after each color). Leave the fifth piece untinted. Mix the ink into each piece of clay to blend, adding additional color as needed to achieve the desired soft tints. The colors will intensify slightly during baking, so do not tint too strongly.

3 roll out clay and stack

Roll out each of the five pieces to sheets approximately $1/16$" (1.5mm) thick. Roll out $1/2$ oz. (14g) translucent clay as thin as possible and then trim into sheets approximately the same size as the tinted sheets. Stack all the colors, alternating the translucent sheets between each layer of color.

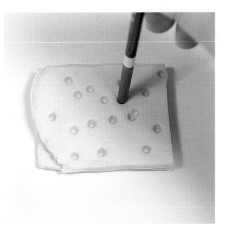

4 compress clay

Compress and stretch the stack by passing an acrylic roller over the clay several times to reduce the thickness of the stack by half.

5 reduce thickness of clay

Use a clay blade to cut the stack down the center into two equal halves. Place one half on top of the other, then again compress and stretch the stack with the roller to reduce the thickness by 50 percent. Cut in half again and stack.

6 drive holes into clay

With the handle end of a paintbrush or another similar tool, drive holes into—but not completely through—the top of the stack. Turn the slab over and drive holes into the bottom in the same manner.

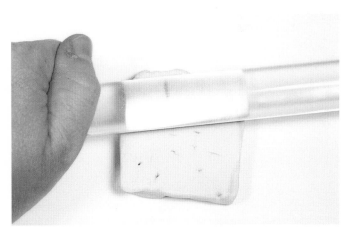

7 compress clay

Holding the slab in your hand with your fingers around the edges, gently compress the sides of the clay toward the center until all the holes on both sides close up.

8 roll out clay slab

Using an acrylic roller, lightly roll the clay to square up the slab.

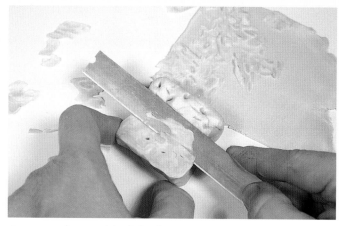

9 cover sheet with slab pieces

Using a clay blade, carefully shave thin pieces off the surface of the stacked slab, keeping the pieces as thin as possible. Roll out the remaining sixth piece of pearl clay into a sheet 1/16" (1.5mm) thick. Lay the shaved pieces onto the pearl sheet until the surface is covered.

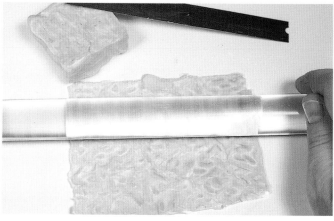

10 secure pieces to sheet

Pass an acrylic rod over the sheet until all the shaved pieces are firmly in place on the sheet.

11 roll and bake sheet

Roll the sheet through the pasta machine to a thickness of 1/16" (1.5mm). At this point, the sheet should be at least 3" × 6" (8cm × 15cm). Bake. Wet-sand the clay sheet, beginning with the 400-grit sandpaper and ending with the 600-grit.

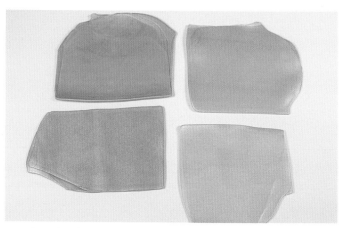

12 tint clay for paua shell sheet

Divide the remaining 2 oz. (57g) pearl clay into four flat pieces. Tint the clay using one of the following combinations of inks for each piece: Sapphire Blue and Shadow Grey; Passion Purple and Burro Brown; Lime Green and Baja Blue; Señorita Magenta, Havana Brown and Burro Brown. Blend the color into each piece completely.

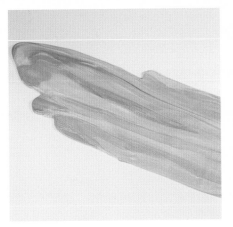

13 twist and slice clay

Roll out each of the four pieces into sheets approximately ⅛" (3mm) thick. Stack and twist the sheets roughly together into a rope or log. Slice in half lengthwise, then stack and twist again.

14 roll out stack

Roll the twisted mass with an acrylic rod to a ¼" (6mm) slab. Then roll the clay through the pasta machine to a thickness of ⅟₁₆" (1.5mm).

15 roll out remaining clay

Roll out the remaining ½ oz. (14g) translucent clay as thin as possible. Lay the translucent sheet on top of the multicolored sheet.

16 paint sheet

Turn the double-layered sheet over so that the translucent clay is on the bottom. Using the flat paintbrush, apply an acrylic paint mixture composed of equal parts Burnt Umber and black to the surface of the multicolored clay sheet. Let dry thoroughly.

17 stack and compress clay

Cut the double-layered sheet into five or six pieces and stack. Roll the stack with an acrylic rod to compress to a thickness of ¼" (6mm). Cut and stack again so that the slab has about twelve striped layers.

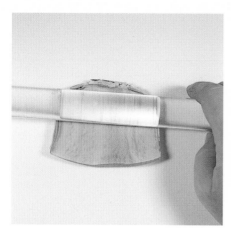

18 roll stack

Pass an acrylic roller over the clay to thin the stack slightly.

19 drive holes into clay

With the handle end of a paintbrush or another similar tool, drive holes into—but not completely through—one side of the clay. Turn the slab over and drive holes into the other side in the same manner.

20 compress clay

Holding the slab in your hand with your fingers around the edges, gently compress the sides of the clay toward the center until all the holes on both sides close up.

21 cover sheet with pieces from slab

Roll out the ½ oz. (14g) black clay into a sheet approximately ¹/₁₆" (1.5mm) thick. Using a clay blade, carefully shave thin pieces off the surface of the stacked slab. Lay the shaved pieces onto the black sheet until the surface is covered.

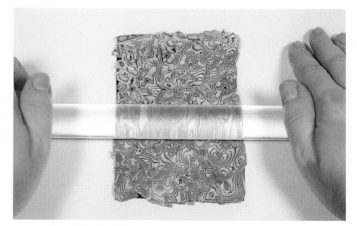

22 roll and bake sheet

Pass an acrylic rod over the sheet until the pieces are firmly in place. Roll the sheet through the pasta machine to a thickness of ¹/₁₆" (1.5mm). The sheet should be at least 3" × 6" (8 cm × 15cm). Bake. Wet-sand the clay sheet, beginning with the 400-grit sandpaper and progressing to the 600-grit.

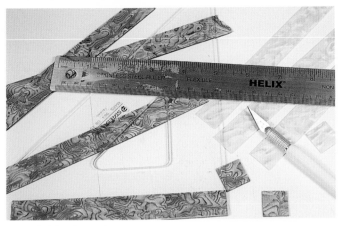

23 divide sheet into squares

With a metal ruler and a right angle, mark both sheets into thirty-two ¾" (2cm) squares. Use the ruler and a craft knife to carefully cut the squares apart.

24 attach squares to box lid

Arrange the squares on the lid of the wooden box into eight columns and eight rows, alternating the mother-of-pearl with the paua shell to create a checkerboard design. Glue the squares in place with a strong white craft glue. Let glue dry completely.

25 varnish board

Varnish the checkerboard, the outside wood surfaces and all the edges. Apply a second coat to the checkerboard after the first is thoroughly dry.

Once the mother-of-pearl and paua shell checkerboard is complete, you are ready to move on to the checker set.

CHECKERS

Jade is translucent with subtle and gradual color changes, while malachite features a stark color contrast with random stripes. In the following steps, you'll be making two kinds of checkers, each in a slightly different way in order to achieve these different effects. The first method (steps 1–4) creates the vein of "minerals" in the jade, while the second method (steps 10–13) creates the obvious striping of the malachite.

1 make molds from buttons
Mix a pea-sized ball of each part of the silicone molding compound until the color is uniform. Press the geometric-patterned button into the compound and let it sit until the mold is firm, about 30 minutes. Repeat the process with the heraldic-patterned button.

2 create sheet of marbled clay for jade checkers
Roll out the translucent clay into a sheet approximately ⅛" (3mm) thick. Brush a light layer of Rainforest Green ink onto the surface of the clay sheet. Let the paint dry. Fold, twist and roll the sheet several times to mix and marble the color. Don't blend the color completely.

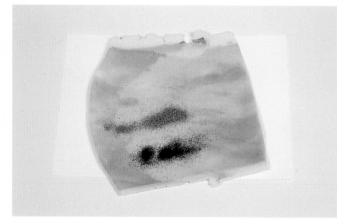

3 add embossing powder
Lay the ⅛" (3mm) clay sheet out flat. Sprinkle the embossing powder onto the sheet in separate piles.

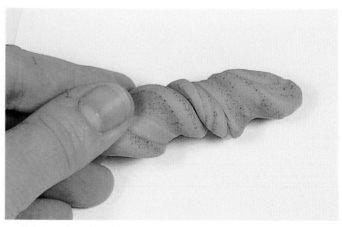

4 fold and twist clay
Use your hands to fold and twist the sheet several times, incorporating the powder into the clay. Do not blend the powder completely into the clay; allow some of the color to appear as streaks.

5 press clay between molds

Smooth and compress the clay into a log approximately ½" (13mm) in diameter. Using a clay blade, cut the log into twelve equal pieces. Press each piece firmly between the two button molds, allowing any excess clay to squeeze out the sides.

6 bake clay checker pieces

Carefully remove clay from the molds. Don't try to trim the excess clay from the edges, as the clay is too soft at this point and will easily be distorted. Bake.

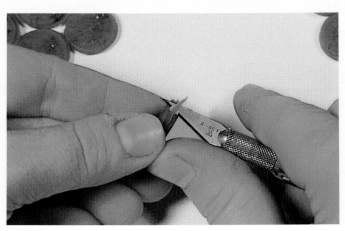

7 trim checkers

While the checkers are still warm, use a craft knife to carefully trim the excess from the edges.

8 apply ink to checkers

Mix a drop or two of black and green ink to create dark green. Lightly brush the dark green ink over the surface of the checkers. With a paper towel, wipe off excess ink from the raised areas of the patterns. Work quickly as the alcohol evaporates and the ink dries rapidly.

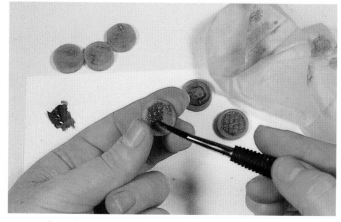

9 apply paint to checkers

Lightly brush the Quinacridone Gold acrylic paint over the surface of the checkers. With a paper towel, remove excess paint from the raised areas. Let the paint dry completely.

10 mix remaining clay for malachite checkers

Mix the green clay, red clay, and ½ oz. (14g) turquoise clay to create a uniform dark forest green. Divide the mixed clay into thirds. Keep one third as is, then mix the marble-sized ball of turquoise clay into another third, and the marble-sized ball of black clay into the remaining third.

11 roll and stack clay

Roll each of the three colors into sheets and stack the sheets roughly.

12 twist clay

Stretch, cut and stack the pile of clay sheets four to five times until the grain, or the thickness of the stripes, is fairly fine. Twist the clay into a rough log, approximately 4" (10cm) in length.

13 roll out clay into sheet

Roll an acrylic rod across the log to flatten it and expose the color striations. Continue to roll out the clay into a sheet approximately 3/16" (5mm) thick.

14 cut and bake checkers

Use a ½" (13mm) circle die to cut out twelve pieces from the clay sheet. As with the jade checkers, press each piece firmly between the two button molds, allowing excess clay to squeeze out the sides. Bake. Carefully trim excess clay from the edges while the pieces are still slightly warm.

15 apply paint to checkers

Brush each checker piece with Verdigris acrylic paint. With a paper towel, wipe off excess paint from the raised areas of the patterns. Let the paint dry completely. Repeat with the gold metallic acrylic paint.

Now that you've finished the jade and malachite game pieces, your set is complete. You're ready for a game of checkers!

PROJECTS INSPIRED BY fabrics
and textiles

Have you ever fallen in love with a fabric simply because its design was so wonderful? If so, try these polymer clay projects that draw inspiration from fabulous fabrics. In this section, we'll focus on pattern as the most significant element of design. Printed in repeat or woven into the material, pattern can be one of the most exciting features about fabric. We'll take into consideration the many components of a pattern, including color, motif, network and scale.

If you have never given the issue of scale much thought before, consider it now. As you work, pay attention to the scale of the pattern as it relates to the overall form. Most of these projects include canework, and the caning process automatically sets the motif into a repeat network. It is easy to get carried away reducing the cane and repeating the pattern, but remember that the scale of the pattern should be proportional to the object and pleasing to the eye.

Project Contributed by ELLEN MARSHALL

african
votive holder

The source for this project is West African Adinkra cloth, which features symbols that are traditionally stamped or screenprinted onto the material. Stamping is useful for this polymer clay project, too, as it provides a quick and easy method of incorporating symbols into the design. If you can't find the right stamps at the store, you can substitute cane slices for stamps by creating canes imitating the symbols, then applying slices of the canes to the form. Ellen Marshall further developed the Adinkra cloth theme with her color scheme and sponge-texture treatment, elements of design that you can easily change if you desire.

materials and tools

- 4 oz. (113g) black clay
- 1 oz. (28g) ecru or beige clay
- 1 oz. (28g) white clay
- 1 oz. (28g) copper metallic clay
- 1 oz. (28g) gold metallic clay
- liquid polymer clay or white craft glue
- metallic liquid acrylic paint: copper (I used Lumiere)
- black ink pad (I used Brilliance)
- glass votive candle holder, 2¾" (7cm) square
- rubber stamps: African Adinkra motifs
- acrylic rod or brayer
- clay blade
- sea sponge

INSPIRATION: AFRICAN SYMBOLS ON ADINKRA CLOTH

Ellen Marshall was inspired by the motifs that appear on Adinkra cloth, a fabric worn as a garment by members of some West African cultures. In these cultures, the Adinkra cloth is a significant object, bearing colors and stamped symbols that relate to important cultural concepts, proverbs and folk stories. The symbols often reveal something about the wearer of the cloth.

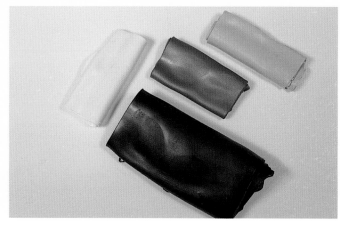

1 condition and blend clay
Condition and roll out the clays. Blend the copper and gold clays together into a medium metallic shade.

2 cover votive holder with clay
Sponge metallic paint onto the rim of the votive holder and let dry. Roll 3 oz. (85g) of black clay into a sheet 1/16" (1.5mm) thick, long enough to wrap around the holder and wide enough to cover the height of the holder. Press the clay onto the holder and smooth the seam. Press any air bubbles toward the bottom and fold the excess clay over the bottom edge.

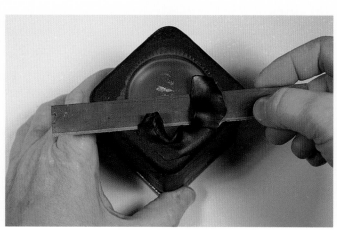

3 even out bottom surface
Using a clay blade, shave the excess clay from the bottom of the votive holder to create an even surface. Press the holder to your work surface to check that the bottom is level.

4 apply metallic paint to surface
Sponge metallic paint onto the surface of the black clay. Set aside for the paint to dry.

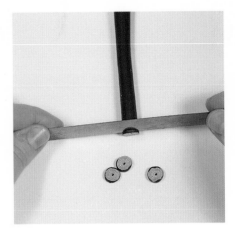

5   stamp clay squares

Roll the ecru and the copper-gold mix into sheets ¹⁄₁₆" (1.5mm) thick. Mark each sheet into 1" (2.5cm) squares. With black ink, use the rubber stamp to apply a design to the center of four squares of each color. Make extra squares in case some stamps do not come out clear. Set the squares aside for the ink to dry. Bake. Cut the squares apart.

6   roll black and white clay

Roll 1 oz. (28g) each of black and white clay into sheets of equal size and ¹⁄₁₆" (1.5mm) thick. Stack the two sheets together and roll them up into a jelly roll.

7   slice black and white clay

Roll the black and white jelly roll to reduce and lengthen the cane until it is approximately ½" (13mm) in diameter. Slice off eight pieces ¹⁄₁₆" (1.5mm) thick.

8   apply accent pieces to votive holder

Apply a small dot of liquid clay or craft glue on the back of all the clay pieces. Gently press the pieces onto each side of the votive holder, arranging them in groups of four. Bake the holder for 30 minutes.

Light a candle inside the votive holder and you have the perfect accent for any room of the house.

snails' trails
quilt pin

Jenny Patterson makes quilt canes, then turns her canes into jewelry and sells them at quilt shows across the country. Jenny gives her quilt canes movement, interest and a fabriclike texture by "messing up" Skinner blend canes and running them through the clay extruder. If you have ever quilted or are familiar with quilts, you know that straight seams and square corners are very much preferred. Using a clay extruder to keep all components regular, you will be able to achieve this ideal. Jenny recommends Fimo Classic for its firmness, but feel free to use a brand with which you are familiar. Just make sure that all your colors have the same consistency, as this will ensure a successful cane.

materials and tools

- 2¼ oz. (64g) beige clay and 2¼ oz. (64g) white clay
- ¾ oz. (21g) camel clay and ¾ oz. (21g) beige clay
- 1¼ oz. (35g) dark red clay and 1¼ oz. (35g) rose clay
- ¾ oz. (21g) dark green clay and ¾ oz. (21g) pale green clay
- 2½ oz. (71g) clay in one of the above colors to use as a border
- pin back
- cyanoacrylate glue
- caulking gun adapted for an extruder
- clay extruder with square and triangular discs
- needle tool or pounce wheel (optional)
- pasta machine

INSPIRATION: QUILT PATTERNS

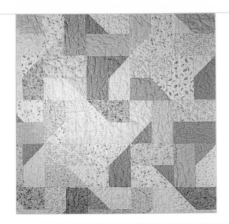

Over the past several years, Jenny Patterson has found much inspiration in quilt patterns. She is always on the lookout for new and challenging designs. This design is called either "Snails' Trails" or "Monkey Wrench," depending on which part of the country you are from. (She happens to like "Snails' Trails.") Once you have mastered the Snails' Trails pattern, all kinds of other designs will pop into your head!

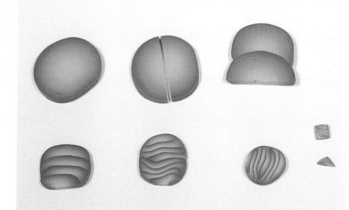

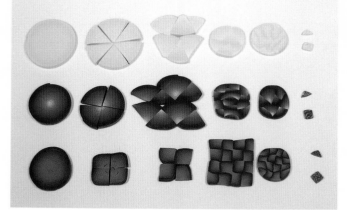

1 create Skinner blends

Create four Skinner blends using the pairs of colors listed on page 55. Roll the blends into spiral canes, lighter color side first. Start with the camel-beige cane and follow the progression shown along the top row, beginning with the Skinner blend (far left). Cut the cane into two lengths (center), restack (right), then reduce the cane to twice its length, cut stack and reduce (bottom row, left). Repeat, reducing the cane to ½" (13mm) diameter, following the progression shown along the bottom row. Cut the cane into lengths to fit into the extruder.

2 create rods

With the remaining Skinner blend canes, follow the progressions shown above. Reassemble and reduce the canes. Extrude the following number of 3" (8cm) long square and triangular rods: • beige/white: 24 square and 16 triangular • camel/beige: 7 square and 8 triangular • red/rose: 9 square and 10 triangular • dark green/light green: 4 square and 6 triangular.

> NOTE
>
> A 3" (8cm) log inserted into the clay gun will yield a square log approximately 12" (30cm) long. A 3½" (9cm) log will yield a triangular rod approximately 36" (91cm) long.

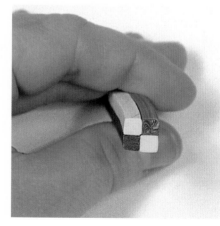

3 create center square

Arrange one green, one red and two white square rods in a checkerboard fashion.

> NOTE
>
> The slices in the images for steps 1–10 represent canes of clay. Slices are shown to easily illustrate how the canes in each step are arranged.

4 begin pattern

Place two white triangular rods together to form a larger right triangle. Repeat with two more white triangular rods, then with two red and with two camel rods. Arrange the four larger right triangles around the center square, with the white opposite each other and the red and camel opposite each other.

5 add triangles

Add another layer of larger triangles around the perimeter, as shown. This time, create the triangles by combining two triangular rods with a square rod.

6 add more triangles

Make red and green right triangles using one square and two triangular rods of each color. Add to the sides of the center square. Add one smaller white triangle, consisting of one square rod and two triangular rods, to the red triangle and one to the green triangle, as shown.

7 add wedges

Build a white wedge with nine square rods and add two triangular rods to the end. Add to one side. Build another wedge and add to the other side.

8 complete pattern

Complete the square by adding one large red and one large camel triangular rod, built from nine squares and four triangles. Compress to consolidate the cane.

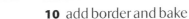

9 cut and reduce cane

Using squeezing force with occasional rolling to keep the sides square and corners sharp, reduce the cane until it is approximately 12" (30cm) long. Cut the cane into four equal pieces and arrange into a square, then compress and reduce the cane again. Cut the cane into four equal pieces, then stack the four pieces into a square again.

10 add border and bake

Roll the remaining clay reserved for the border into a ¼" (6mm) thick sheet. Wrap the sheet around the cane to create a border. Cut slices ¹⁄₁₆" (1.5mm) thick and press each slice lightly between two pieces of fabric to add a subtle texture. If desired, simulate stitching lines with a needle tool or a pounce wheel.

To make the "quilt" into a pin, attach the pin back to the back of the base with cyanoacrylate glue. Cover the pin back with a bead of liquid polymer clay, then press a small strip of clay onto the pin-back body for a neatly finished piece. To make a pair of matching earrings, simply attach findings to the back of two "quilts."

silk tie pattern
business accessories set

Patterned silk ties are a valuable—not to mention easily-accessible—source of inspiration. Many tie patterns are composed of identical units that are repeated throughout the fabric. This repetition of units is called a *design network*. Once the unit is designed, you can choose your own network to create the look you want. When developing your network, consider the scale of the pattern units as well as the contrast in value and color. A pleasing pattern results when these elements are in harmony.

materials and tools

- ¼ oz. (7g) black
- ½ oz. (14g) light brown clay
- 1 oz. (28g) navy clay
- 1 oz. (28g) rose clay
- 1 oz. (28g) white or cream clay
- colored pencils
- business accessories: business card case, money clip, pen with brass tubing, key chain with brass tubing
- silk tie with pleasing pattern
- cyanoacrylate glue
- water-based varnish (optional)
- acrylic rod or brayer
- brass tubing, approximately ⅜" (9mm) diameter, 6"–8" (15cm–20cm) long
- clay blade
- jeweler's lathe or rotary tool, fitted with muslin wheel
- pasta machine
- wet-dry sandpaper, 400- and 600-grit (800-grit optional)
- 2 index cards
- sketch paper

INSPIRATION: SILK TIES

I enjoy buying ties for my husband. If I leave it up to him, he picks wide-striped patterns—ugh. When he wears the ones I choose, he always receives compliments! I have to admit that I have specific criteria for selecting his ties beyond just fashion—I've got to be able to cane the patterns!

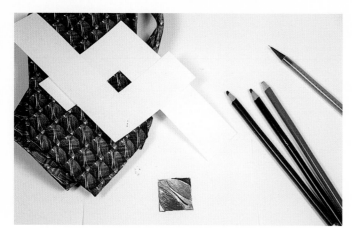

1 sketch pattern unit

Cut two index cards into L shapes. Use these to create a viewing window, then isolate the repeated unit of the pattern on the tie. With colored pencils, create a sketch of the pattern in a scale approximately the size at which the initial cane will be developed.

2 create Skinner blends

Create Skinner blends of the colors that you have chosen to use in the pattern.

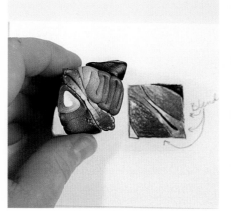

3 reproduce unit with clay

Roll, fold or stack the blends to roughly approximate the color gradations and shapes in the pattern unit.

4 add details to clay unit

Add additional lines or shapes to the clay unit. (In the photo above, the black line down the center of the tan shape has been inserted.) Begin to consolidate the pieces into a cane and work it into a square.

5 reduce the cane

Reduce the cane by compressing, stretching and rolling it with the acrylic rod to maintain the square corners. Trim the distorted ends and check the pattern against your original sketch. Reduce the cane to the desired size.

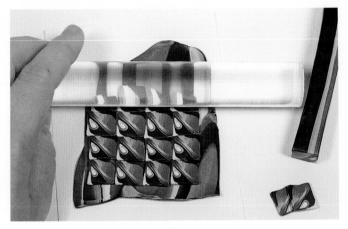

6 create square network sheet

Create a backing sheet by rolling the trimmed scraps into a sheet ¹⁄₁₆"
(1.5mm) thick. Cut ¹⁄₁₆" (1.5mm) slices from the end of the cane and
arrange them on the backing sheet, orienting the pattern units in the
same direction and butting all the edges closely together. This pattern
is a simple square network (see *Networks*, page 62). With the acrylic rod,
roll the sheet to blend the seams, as shown here. Roll the sheet through
the pasta machine to ¹⁄₁₆" (1.5mm) thickness, rotating the sheet 90
degrees as necessary to maintain the square pattern.

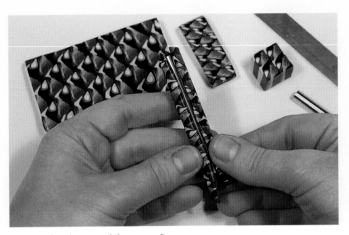

7 apply clay to object surfaces

Using the clay blade, cut shapes from the sheet to fit the top of the
business card case and money clip. Gently press the clay onto the
object surfaces, taking care not to leave fingerprints. Cut the sheet to
the length and circumference of the brass tubes of the pen and the
key-chain. Wrap the clay around the tubes.

8 bake, sand and finish clay

Gently roll a piece of brass tubing across the clay to blend the seams.
Bake all the pieces. Carefully separate the clay sheets from the business card case and money clip, then reapply them after adding
cyanoacrylate glue to the back of the sheets. Sand all the clay surfaces
with 400-, 600- and, if desired, 800-grit sandpaper, taking care not to
sand across the brass areas. Buff with a muslin wheel or apply two or
three coats of water-based varnish.

Any businessperson is sure to make a good impression with this
matching accessories set.

NETWORKS

In the textile industry, units of pattern are repeated and printed across a piece of cloth. The arrangement in which the unit or motif is placed is known as a *network*. For a square or rectangular unit, there can be several basic types of networks.

 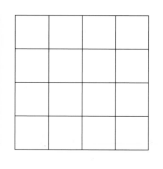

square network

The square units are repeated in perfect vertical and horizontal rows to form a gridlike design.

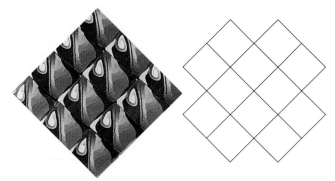

diamond network

Like the square network, the square units are placed in regular vertical and horizontal rows. The entire network, however, is rotated 45 degrees to turn the squares into diamonds.

 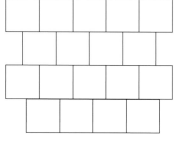

brick network

The square units are lined up in horizontal rows. The rows are then staggered, giving the appearance of laid bricks.

 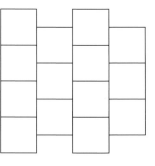

half-drop network

The square units are lined up in vertical rows. The rows are then staggered, so that every other row looks as if it has dropped.

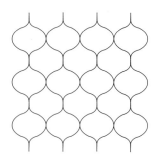

ogee pattern   scale pattern

other networks

Shapes other than squares and rectangles also may be placed in repeat, such as triangles, ogees, hexagons and semicircles. Pictured above at left is an ogee network, which consists of shapes formed by tangent S-shaped curves. At right is a scale network, featuring a repetition of semicircles that gives the appearance of fish scales.

TIP

The more complex repeats such as half-drop or brick networks, as well as the combination of mirrored and reversed cane slices (see page 63), create a myriad of possible patterns. However, designs tend to be more pleasing to the eye when the unit and pattern of the repeat are easily read. Keep the scale of the project in mind when designing any repeat pattern so that there will be room for several units to appear within the piece.

NETWORKS IN USE

reversing the unit

You can develop further variations with the cane design by alternately reversing the pattern unit. This pattern alternates the unit's orientation to repeat the mirror image across each row.

mirroring the unit

This pattern alternates mirroring the unit across each row and down each row. Ultimately, a larger motif unit is created.

irregular silk tie patterns

This clay "fabric" was developed in two stages. First, the irregularly shaped cane was designed and created, then repeated in a manner similar to that of a scale network. Next, the circular cane slices were added and rolled on.

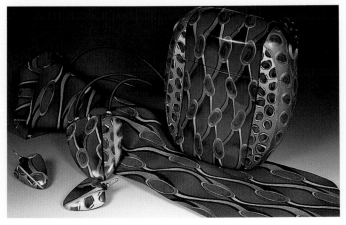

evening purse and jewelry set

To create this little evening purse and jewelry set, coordinating patterns were developed to harmonize with the main pattern.

patterns for narrow pieces

Black clay and two Skinner blends form the basis for this pattern. The cane was developed from the stacked blends. Since the pattern couldn't be set into traditional repeat, the slices were laid on the backing sheet and stretched in only one direction to keep the pattern small. This type of pattern works well for narrow pieces such as bracelets or hair barrettes.

coordinate prints
jewelry set

To make this necklace and earring set, you will be creating sheets of clay inspired by beautiful, printed fabrics. My sources are rose- and cream-colored fabric designs that offer a variety of interesting patterns. These fabrics have a very small range of value contrast, which means that the pattern in the clay will be subtle. Avoid reducing the canes too much, as this makes the patterns fade out and thus diminishes their readability. With such an incredible selection of fabric available these days, you can adapt the project to fit whatever patterns you find inspirational.

materials and tools

- 4 oz. (113g) cream clay
- 4 oz. (113g) rose clay
- approximately 2 oz. (57g) scrap clay for bead cores
- 30–50 accent beads, gold, stone and/or glass, approximately 3mm and 5mm
- gold earring posts
- gold necklace clasp
- 2 gold bead end caps
- 3–4 fabric samples, such as home décor fabric
- 18k gold leafing pen
- nylon bead thread
- beading needle
- cyanoacrylate glue
- water-based varnish
- acrylic rod or brayer
- brass tubing, approximately ⅜" (9mm) diameter, 6"–8" (15cm–20cm) long
- clay blade
- circle cutters, 1¼" (3cm) diameter and 1½" (4cm) diameter
- needle tool
- pasta machine
- texturing sheet, folded in half
- wet-dry sandpaper, 400- and 600-grit

INSPIRATION: FABRICS

My sister has a custom drapery and upholstery business. Frequently, she saves for me samples of fabrics that have been discontinued by the manufacturers. They are often arranged in the sample books according to color, with families of coordinating prints, to give customers furnishing and decorating ideas. Well, they give *me* ideas, too! Who says you can't mix prints and stripes?!

1 create Skinner blend

Set about ½ oz. (14g) of each solid color clay aside for later use. Create a Skinner blend with the remaining clay. When the blend is satisfactory, rotate the folded sheet one quarter turn, then roll the sheet through the pasta machine to lengthen and spread the shaded blend. Roll several more times, decreasing the thickness setting each time until the sheet is about ¹⁄₁₆" (1.5mm) thick and about 12"–15" (30cm–38cm) long.

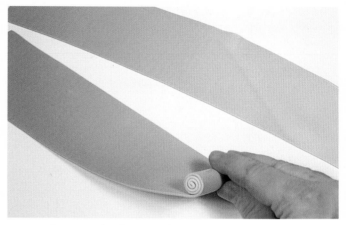

2 cut sheet and roll one strip

Cut the sheet lengthwise into two equal strips. Roll one strip jelly-roll style into a bull's-eye cane, starting with the cream end so that the center is lightest. Set aside for use in step 9.

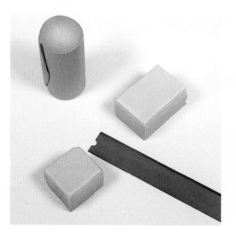

3 stack clay for stripe pattern

For the first pattern, which is striped, cut the other strip widthwise into several equal rectangular pieces, each 1" (2.5cm) wide. Stack the pieces light to dark, with the cream on top. From the stacked block of clay, cut a piece slightly less than half the block. Reserve the other piece for use in step 6.

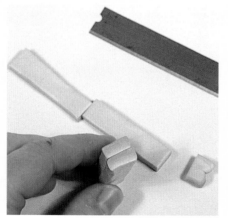

4 compress and reduce stack

Reduce the cane, compressing and stretching the block until it is 8"–10" (20cm–25cm) long. Roll the block with an acrylic rod periodically during the reducing process to maintain even, square corners. Trim any uneven or distorted portions off the ends with a clay blade. Cut the cane into four even pieces and begin to stack the pieces.

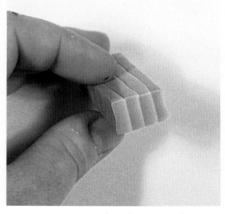

5 compress and reduce stack again

When all four pieces are stacked, compress the stack and reduce it again slightly. Set aside this striped cane until you begin assembling the finished piece.

6 cut block into pieces for geometric patterns

For the second and third patterns, which are geometric, stand the reserved stacked block of clay from step 3 on end. Cut the block lengthwise into five to seven random pieces.

7 arrange pieces into cane

Rearrange the pieces into a new pattern, keeping all the pieces standing on end. Compress the arrangement into a right triangle and reduce the cane to approximately 4½"–5" (11cm–13cm) long.

8 cut and reassemble cane

Using a clay blade, trim the cane ends and divide the cane into two equal lengths, about 2" (5cm) long. Reassemble the cane by placing the two pieces next to each other so that their ends mirror each other and form a triangle.

9 reduce, assemble and compress cane

Reduce the triangle-shaped cane again until it is about 8" (20cm) long, then cut it into four equal lengths. Assemble the four sections so that their ends create a square with a symmetrical design. Compress to consolidate the cane.

Cut a 1" (2.5cm) length from the bull's-eye cane made in step 2 and set aside for the leaf pattern. With the remaining bull's-eye cane, repeat steps 6–9 to create a second geometric pattern.

10 slice bull's-eye cane for leaf pattern

For the fourth pattern, which is a leaf design in repetition, stand the piece of the bull's-eye cane reserved for the leaf in step 9 on end. Slice it lengthwise into four or five parallel pieces. Roll the reserved rose clay to a sheet 1/32" (1mm) thick, then cut pieces from the sheet to fit between each parallel slice.

11 reassemble slices, then cut

Reassemble the slices, then cut the clay in half diagonally across the slices.

12 form leaf

Cut another piece from the rose sheet to fit along the diagonal cut, then insert it between the two halves of the cane. Flip one half over and line its edge along the diagonal division so that the series of cuts on either side now intersect a center line as veins of a leaf. Pinch the sides to form a pointed leaf shape and reduce the cane to about 3/8" (9mm) wide.

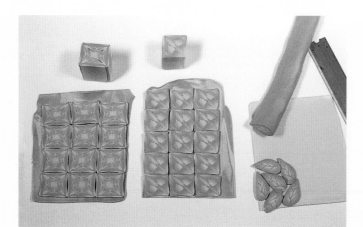

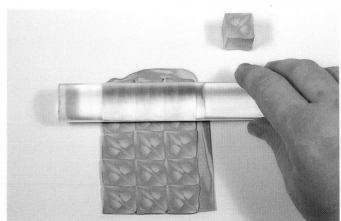

13 apply slices to clay sheets

Collect all the leftover trimmings from the distorted ends, then roll them together into sheets 1/16" (1.5mm) thick. Also roll out any remaining solid colors into sheets 1/16" (1.5mm) thick. Cut 1/16" (1.5mm) thick slices from the ends of each cane and lay them out on the sheets, the square slices butting up tightly together. Lay the leaf slices out randomly. Slice the reserved striped cane lengthwise (not shown). Lay the several striped slices next to each other on a backing sheet.

14 roll sheets flat

Use an acrylic rod to blend the seams and consolidate the pattern on each sheet. Roll each sheet through the pasta machine at the thickest setting, then progress down to 1/16" (1.5mm) thick, rotating the sheet 90 degrees as necessary to maintain an even square pattern. (Do not rotate the striped sheet.)

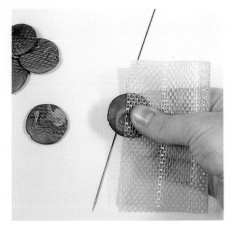

15 create textured bead cores

With scrap clay, form nine lentil-shaped beads approximately 1¼" (3cm) in diameter. Use a needle tool to pierce through the beads, edge to edge. Press a texture sheet onto the surface of each bead, creating an imprint on both sides. Make two smaller, one-sided pieces for earrings. Bake and cool.

16 paint bead cores

Paint the textured areas of the bead cores with the gold leafing pen. Let the gold leaf dry approximately 30 minutes before continuing.

17 apply shapes to bead cores

Using the two circle cutters, cut football and crescent shapes from the patterned clay sheets and apply them to the bead cores. Mix and match the patterns on each of the beads. Allow some of the gold leafing to show through by leaving a space between the patterned shapes.

18 bake and finish

Use the small brass tube to gently roll the seams closed and smooth. Bake, sand and apply two coats of water-based varnish. String the patterned beads and accent beads onto a length of nylon thread, then finish with gold findings on the ends. Use cyanoacrylate glue to attach earring posts to the untextured sides of the two smaller beads.

Patterned bead jewelry can be the finishing touch to an outfit.

PROJECTS INSPIRED BY *jewelry*

Gleaming precious metal, glittering gemstones and lustrous colors give jewelry its irresistible appeal. And while this appeal is universal, we all have our favorites. Gold, enamels and cameos are what catch my eye. I have experimented for several years with different paints and supplies to imitate my favorite looks in jewelry. This has led me to explore many ways to achieve convincing gold effects as well as the glowing, intense, translucent color over gold that is a hallmark of enamelwork.

One of the many benefits of working with polymer clay is that you can create an object that looks like metal without having to struggle with the metal medium and its drawbacks, such as cost, rigidity and working technique. As a result, you have more freedom to explore line, shape and pattern for faux gold effects. So have fun with these jewelry-inspired projects and design extravagantly!

child's
vanity set

The gold finish of this vanity set resembles the characteristic patina of brass costume jewelry, giving it a worn, aged quality. This antique look comes not from the passing of time but from polymer clay know-how! First, you'll fashion a surface, using gold metallic powder over gold clay to achieve depth and warmth. Then, you'll create the antique effect by applying brown and black ink to the recesses of the textured areas. The project steps illustrate how to make a mirror and comb; use the same techniques to create a matching hairbrush or any other objects that you would like to accompany the set.

materials and tools

- 4–6 oz. (113–170g) gold clay (nonmetallic)
- liquid polymer clay
- Piñata inks: Havana Brown and Mantilla Black
- metallic powder: gold
- small oval mirror
- comb (those marked "unbreakable" will withstand baking)
- hairbrush (optional; test in oven first before proceeding)
- cornstarch powder
- 70% isopropyl (rubbing) alcohol
- push molds in flower shapes (I used Sculpey Sconce Décor)
- acrylic rod or brayer
- clay blade
- dust mask
- 2 oval cutters, one slightly larger and one slightly smaller than the mirror
- small paintbrushes, round and detail
- palette
- wooden craft stick, for the mirror handle
- cup for alcohol

INSPIRATION: ANTIQUE GOLD COSTUME JEWELRY

Much "antique gold" costume jewelry is not really gold at all, but brass— perhaps plated with gold. The antique look comes from a darkened patina, particularly in the depths of textured surfaces or on areas where the plating has worn away. If you look closely at this brass bracelet, you can see its fine patina within the textured areas.

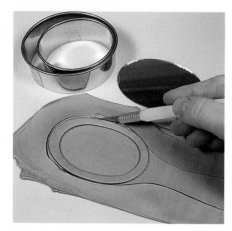

1 cut mirror shape from clay

Roll the gold clay to a ⅛" (3mm) thick sheet. Lay the mirror on the sheet, trace around it and cut the overall shape from the clay to create the base. Repeat to cut a second identical shape. (A paper template may be useful.) Use the oval cutters to cut the frame for the mirror.

2 adhere clay frame to mirror

Lay the mirror on the base, then lay the oval frame over the mirror. Adjust the placement so that the edges of the frame match up with the edges of the base. When the placement is correct, gently lift up the oval frame, apply a bead of liquid clay around the mirror and adhere the frame over the mirror.

3 seal clay frame

Turn the base over, mirror-side down, and apply a liberal amount of liquid clay to the surface. Place the craft stick along the length of the handle and apply the second base-shaped layer of clay on top, sandwiching the stick between the layers. Press all the edges together firmly, sealing out air bubbles. Bake for 20–30 minutes. Cool completely.

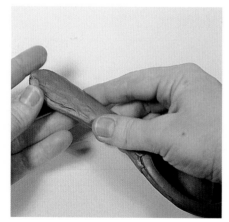

4 add layer to mirror base

Roll a sheet of gold clay ¹⁄₁₆" (1.5mm) thick. Wrap this sheet around the mirror base, enclosing all cut edges and forming a smooth surface. Blend all seams and smooth out the clay, dusting the clay and your hands periodically with cornstarch powder to eliminate bumps, fingerprints and other imperfections on the clay.

5 create design elements

Press pieces of gold clay into the molds. Use a clay blade to shave away the excess so that the clay is even with the surface of the tray, then remove the piece from the mold.

6 add design elements

Assemble an ornamental design on the back of the mirror, using several flowers, leaves or other elements. Apply a small bead of liquid clay to the back of each element and press gently onto the clay surface.

7 apply metallic powder

With a small paintbrush, apply metallic powder to the entire surface of the mirror, front and back, including the ornamental designs. Bake for 30 minutes.

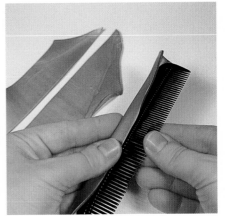

8 cover and embellish comb

Roll out a 1/16" (1.5mm) thick sheet of gold clay and cut a strip wide enough to cover the comb handle. Fold the strip over the handle, covering both sides, and press firmly to the surface. Cut the ends, butt the edges together, then blend the seam. Embellish as with the mirror. Apply metallic powder over the entire clay surface and bake.

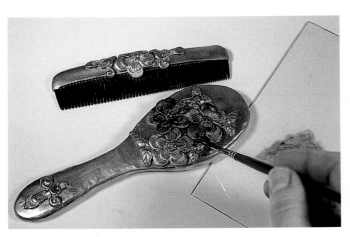

9 antique surfaces

Mix black and brown inks on a palette and thin with a small amount of rubbing alcohol. Using a paintbrush, apply this mixture over the metallic surface, heavily in some places and lightly in others to give the objects an aged and distressed look.

To complete the set, cover a hairbrush with polymer clay and apply the same surface treatment.

cameo
brooch

Cameos are not the only source of inspiration for this project. An additional source is Wedgwood's famous white-on-blue porcelain. Unlike cameo white, Wedgwood white is fairly opaque. Feel free to draw inspiration from either cameos or Wedgwood—or both—in your use of opaque and translucent white clay. You will be creating a leaf from this white clay, and you have the option of reusing the mold that you made for the Leaf Fossil Pendant and Box project (pages 30–35). If you've skipped ahead and you passed over that project, or if your mold is too big, go back and make a new mold using the same technique.

materials and tools

- 1 oz. (28g) white clay (may be solid white or a mixture of white, pearl and/or translucent, as desired)
- ½ oz. (14g) Ultramarine Blue clay
- ¼ oz. (7g) pearl clay
- ¼ oz. (7g) white clay
- pea-sized ball of black clay
- liquid polymer clay
- leaf mold from Leaf Fossil Pendant and Box project (see page 32, steps 1–3)
- pin back
- cyanoacrylate glue
- cornstarch powder
- acrylic rod or brayer
- circle cutter, approximately 2½" (6cm) diameter
- craft knife
- pasta machine
- pointed tools such as dental picks or sculptor's tools
- wet-dry sandpaper, 400-, 600- and 800-grit
- burned-out small floodlight bulb or other domed form

INSPIRATION: CAMEO BROOCH

True cameo jewelry is crafted from layered agate or shell. The translucent light color is carefully and selectively carved away, revealing the darker layer of color beneath. Contrasting with the darker background, the light-colored design sits in high relief.

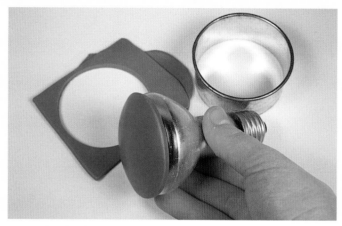

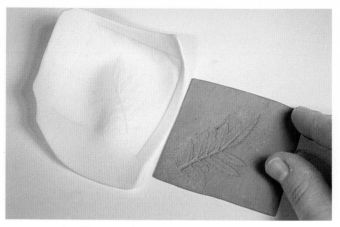

1 make the base

Mix the Ultramarine Blue clay with ¼ oz. (7g) pearl clay, ¼ oz. (7g) white clay and the ball of black clay to a consistent Wedgwood Blue color, then roll out a sheet ¼" (6mm) thick with the acrylic rod. Using the circle cutter, cut out a circle from the sheet. Gently press the circle onto the domed surface of the light bulb. Bake on the lightbulb, then wet-sand the surface and edges of the clay, starting with the 400-grit sandpaper and progressing to the 800-grit.

2 create leaf impression

Roll out the white clay to a thickness appropriate for use with the leaf mold (see pages 32–33). Sprinkle a liberal amount of cornstarch powder over the clay sheet to eliminate all tackiness. Roll the clay and mold together through the pasta machine on the widest setting. Carefully peel the clay sheet and the mold apart.

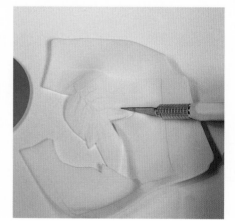

3 cut out leaf impression

Using a craft knife, cut around the leaf impression to remove it from the sheet. Do not cut right to the edge of the design; allow at least ⅛" (3mm) of space around the entire perimeter of the impression.

4 apply liquid polymer clay

Turn the leaf piece over and apply a bead of liquid polymer clay on the back side, along the center of the leaf and approximately along the vein lines. Use the liquid clay sparingly, as you do not want it to ooze beyond the leaf shape onto the base.

5 apply leaf to base

Apply the leaf impression to the base piece. With a pointed tool such as a dental pick, cut along the leaf edges in downward, outward strokes. Each cut should seal the leaf edge to the base surface.

6 add detail
Try various tools to achieve the effect of different lines and shapes along the edge of the leaf. Continue to cut away all the extra white background clay around the leaf.

7 finish leaf and bake
Cut away any interior spaces between the leaves. To create texture and accentuate the delicacy of the molded image, carve out some depth within the leaf impression. Clean up all the edges by removing any liquid clay or remnants of solid clay on the base. Bake.

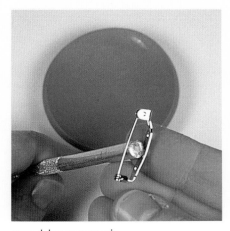

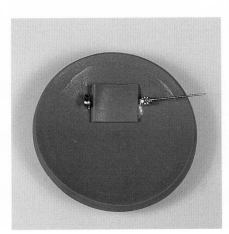

8 add curve to pin
With a rounded tool such as the end of a pen or craft knife, gently add a slight curve to the base of the pin back.

9 attach and secure pin
Attach the pin to the back of the base with cyanoacrylate glue. Cover the pin back with a bead of liquid polymer clay, then press a small strip of matching blue clay onto the pin back body for a neatly finished piece.

Accessorize your outfit by wearing your very own cameo brooch.

cloisonné enamel
pendant and earrings

In true cloisonné enamelwork, a pattern of raised lines is created by soldering fine wire to a metal base plate, usually made of silver or gold. These raised lines function as walls, which form repository cells for each enamel color. In this project, clay takes the place of metal. Instead of a metal base plate, you'll roll out a sheet of clay. And, using a clay extruder fitted with the smallest circle die, you'll make clay "wires," which will be applied to the sheet to make cells. The cells will then be filled with tinted liquid clay to imitate the rich colors and translucent quality of enamel.

materials and tools

- 1–2 oz. (28-57g) scrap clay
- 1 oz. (28g) black clay (or another color to coordinate with the surface design)
- 1 oz. (28 g) gold metallic clay
- liquid polymer clay
- Piñata inks: several colors of your choice
- two-part epoxy resin
- cyanoacrylate glue
- 23k gold leaf
- necklace closure findings
- french earwires with leg
- 2–4 accent beads
- 19-gauge gold wire, 4" (10cm) long

- Buna cord (nitrile rubber), 20–24" (51–61cm) long, with 2 end caps to fit cord
- scrap wire
- acrylic rod or brayer
- clay blade
- clay extruder
- craft knife
- hand drill with a 0.7mm bit
- heat gun
- needle-nose pliers
- needle tool
- oval cutters ³⁄₄" × 1" (2cm × 2.5cm) and 1½" × 2" (4cm × 5cm), or desired size

- paintbrush (wide, very soft)
- palette (glass or Plexiglas)
- palette knife (plastic)
- sanding sponge, medium-grit
- disposable cup and stir stick for resin

ADDITIONAL MATERIALS FOR CHAMPLEVÉ PROJECT:

- rubber stamp
- rubber-tipped tool, such as Color Shapers
- post earring findings

INSPIRATION: CLOISONNÉ ENAMELWORK

In the art of cloisonné, the wire designs can be applied to many surfaces, including jewelry and beads, decorative ornaments and functional pieces such as this stamp dispenser. The variation on page 85 is inspired by the related art of champlevé, in which the enamel fills incised or hollowed-out areas on the base.

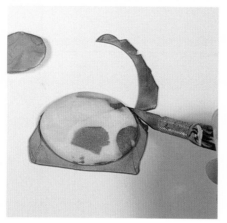

1 create base forms

With scrap clay of any color, roll out a clay sheet ⅛" (3mm) thick. Use the oval cutters to cut two small ovals and one large oval. Bevel the edges of each oval form. Bake.

2 cover forms with clay

Roll gold clay into a sheet 1/16" (1.5mm) thick. With a craft knife, cut ovals to fit the flat sides of the base forms. Press the gold clay firmly onto the form.

3 texture clay surface

Texture the gold clay surface by impressing it into a sanding sponge.

4 create design on surface

Using the smallest die with the clay extruder, extrude a piece of clay about 12" (30cm) long. Arrange the extrusion into a desired design on the gold surface of each oval piece, then gently press down on the extrusion so that it adheres to the surface.

5 apply gold leaf

Cut small pieces of gold leaf to fit over the oval shapes. Apply the gold leaf to the clay surface and gently press or rub the leaf until it is released from the carrier sheet onto the clay. With a soft brush, use a downward tapping motion to press the gold leaf into the recessed areas of the clay surface. Bake for 30 minutes and cool completely.

6 mix and apply colors

Mix a palette of colors with liquid polymer clay and inks (see *Tip*, below). Blend two shades of each desired color; if using violet, for example, mix red-violet and blue-violet. Within each closed section of the design, fill one side of the section with one shade and the other side with the other shade, using the plastic palette knife to apply the ink.

7 blend colors on surface

With the palette knife, draw one shade into the other, creating a gradual progression. To avoid inadvertent color mixing, set the liquid clay with a heat gun before proceeding to the next cell. To do so, place the pieces on a heat-resistant surface, then heat them until the liquid becomes matte and then slightly shiny again, with gold reflecting through it.

8 finish applying colors and bake

Repeat steps 6 and 7 with any other color combinations, again mixing two shades of color and then blending them into each other on the gold leaf surface. When the surface is covered, bake again for 20 minutes.

9 apply black clay and bake

Roll out the black clay to a sheet 3/32" (2mm) thick. Press the sheet onto the back of the ovals, wrapping it around to the front, over the beveled edges. Use a clay blade to cut away the excess clay, trimming the clay level with the front surface. Bake for 30 minutes.

TIP

To mix colors, first squeeze several donut-shaped circles of liquid polymer clay onto the palette. Add one or two drops of ink into each circle and stir to combine. Allow the clay and ink mixture to rest on the palette so that the alcohol will evaporate (otherwise, the mixture will bubble when you apply it to the gold leaf surface). After 20 or 30 minutes, the colors can be applied directly to the surface, or they can be mixed with each other on the palette to create an unlimited array of colors.

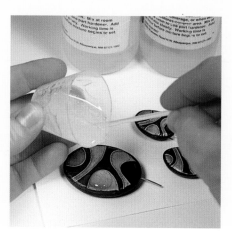

10 drill holes for findings

Using a hand drill, drill one hole into the top, center edge of each oval to accommodate the jewelry findings. Insert scrap wire into the holes for temporary handles.

11 coat with epoxy resin

Mix the epoxy resin according to package directions. Carefully pour the resin onto the surface of the three forms, adding enough resin to create a smooth, level surface. With a disposable stir stick, draw the resin to the very edge of the surface, but not over it. Let the resin set and cure according to the directions. This may be up to 24 hours.

12 add beaded wire loops

Remove the scrap wire from the drilled holes. With a pair of needle-nose pliers, create a small hangman's loop with gold wire. Add accent beads to the gold wire, then use cyanoacrylate glue to secure the wire into the drilled hole of the pendant. Add accent beads to the french earwires, then glue the wires into the drilled holes of the earrings.

13 add end caps and findings

Thread the Buna cord through the pendant loop. Glue the cord end caps on each end and add closure findings.

As you are finishing, feel free to personalize your pieces. I "sign" my necklaces by incorporating a name cane bead into the closure.

CHAMPLEVÉ ENAMEL EARRINGS

For this project, you'll create the earring design in the clay with a rubber stamp. If the negative (recessed) portion of the rubber stamp is pleasing and its impression will provide cells to fill with color, use the stamp itself as your mold. If the positive (raised) portion of the stamp is more suitable, make a mold by pressing the stamp into a 3mm thick sheet of Sculpey SuperFlex Bake & Bend clay. Bake and cool the mold.

1 prepare impressions and bake

Powder the surface of a 3/32" (2mm) thick gold clay sheet with cornstarch. Create two impressions by pressing the powdered side of the sheet into the mold. Remove the clay and trim the edges neatly. Apply 23k gold leaf to cover the clay, using a soft brush to press the leaf into recessed areas. Bake for 20 minutes.

2 fill cells with color and bake

Mix liquid polymer clay and ink on the palette (see *Tip*, page 83). Apply color to the cells with a palette knife or needle tool as desired. Use a rubber-tipped tool to wipe any color from the raised gold areas. When the design is filled with color, bake again for 20 minutes.

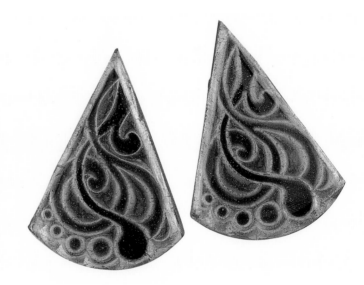

3 add resin coating and wire

Mix the epoxy resin according to the package directions, then pour a small amount onto the surface of each piece, using a disposable stir stick to draw the resin out to the edges. Cover the entire surface with a smooth, level coating, without allowing the resin to run over the edges. Let the resin set and cure, following the package instructions. Assemble the earrings, attaching the post findings to the back of each piece with cyanoacrylate glue.

The technique of champlevé is similar to cloisonné. In champlevé, however, an impression is stamped upon the metal surface, creating cells that are *depressed into* the surface rather than *raised above* the surface.

surprise goose
egg box

The style and design of a Fabergé egg is unmistakable. One of the trademark secrets of the House of Fabergé is the process of enameling over large areas of *guilloche*, a patterned, textured gold. In the late nineteenth century, the famous jeweler Peter Carl Fabergé developed new formulas for colors, including yellows, pinks and greens, expanding the limited palette that had been available to other jewelers of his time. This project not only uses pink and gold to recall the splendor of Fabergé's famous eggs, it uses the ghost image metallic effect to simulate the enameled guilloche field over the surface of the egg. Apply gold leaf and crystals as lavishly as you please to make an exquisite jewel.

materials and tools

- 4 oz. (113g) black clay
- 4 oz. (113g) pearl clay
- dime-sized ball of Alizarin Crimson clay
- 1 oz. (28g) gold metallic clay
- 1 oz. (28g) Sculpey SuperFlex Bake & Bend clay
- liquid polymer clay
- goose egg, emptied of contents (see *Tip*, page 88)
- 23k gold leaf
- 20–30 Austrian crystals, 1mm
- 10–20 Austrian crystals, 2 mm
- textured, small tube bead with a hole in the center

- brass hinge, ¾" × 1" (2cm × 2.5cm)
- cornstarch powder
- cyanoacrylate glue
- water-based varnish
- acrylic rod or brayer
- ceramic tile or glass sheet
- circle cutters, various sizes between 2½" (6cm) and 4" (10cm) diameter
- oval cutters, 3¼" × 4" (8cm × 10cm) and 3½" × 4½" (9cm × 11cm)
- clay blade
- craft knife
- knitting needle (fine, double-pointed)

- needle tool (sharp)
- paintbrushes: one soft and wide for applying gold leaf; one for varnishing
- palette knife (metal)
- pasta machine
- permanent marker
- texturing sheet with a simple linear pattern, such as Scratch Art Shade-Tex
- tweezers
- water mister (optional)
- wet-dry sandpaper, 320-, 400-, 600- and 800-grit

INSPIRATION: FABERGÉ EGGS

Peter Carl Fabergé became the favored jeweler for the Imperial family of Russia between 1885 and 1915. Perhaps the most famous products of his workshop were his Imperial eggs—jeweled, decorated eggs ordered by the czars and given to their wives as gifts at Easter. Inside, the eggs always contained a special surprise.

1 cover egg with black clay

Empty the egg (see *Tip*, below). Roll out a ⅛"
(3mm) thick sheet of black clay. Cut a strip
about ½" (13mm) shorter than the girth of
the egg and 4"–5" (10cm–13cm) wide. Wrap
the strip around the egg, stretching the ends
to meet. Cut two clay circles and fit them
over the top and bottom of the egg. Work
the seams closed with an acrylic rod.

2 mark lid and bake

Mark the lid by lightly pressing an oval cutter into the clay surface. Using the sharp
needle tool, pierce through the large hole in
the shell to allow air to escape while baking.
Bake for 30 minutes. Cool until you are able
to handle the egg.

3 cut lid

While the egg is still slightly warm, cut along
the lid line with a craft knife equipped with
a new, sharp blade. Cut through the clay on
the first pass. Make several subsequent
passes over the lid line, scoring until the
blade cuts through the eggshell.

4 place hinge

With the lid in place, hold the lid and the
egg together, then determine the placement of the hinge. Using the craft knife, cut
out a small, narrow, rectangular opening in
the clay, just large enough to accommodate
the barrel of the hinge.

TIP

To empty an egg of its contents, use a sharp needle tool to pierce the smaller end of the egg, making
a hole approximately ¹⁄₃₂" (1mm) in size. On the opposite end, make a second hole and enlarge it to
nearly ¼" (6mm). Insert the needle into the egg and gently stir the contents to break up the yolk.
Blow through the small hole to drive the contents out of the large hole. Rinse the egg inside and out
with warm water several times and allow it to dry for several days, or for 20–30 minutes in a warm
(200°F/ 93°C) oven.

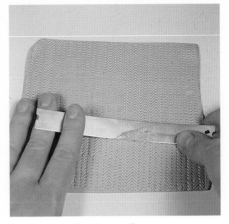

5 secure hinge

Use cyanoacrylate glue to secure the hinge in place. Do not allow the glue to run into the barrel of the hinge, or it will be immobilized. After the glue is dry, add a bit of black clay over each side of the hinge and bevel it outward, creating a smooth slope for the next layer of clay.

6 roll out patterned sheet

Mix the pearl clay with the Alizarin Crimson to make a pink pearl color. Roll the clay through the pasta machine to a $3/32$" (2mm) thickness. Dust the clay with cornstarch as a resist to the texture plate. At the same setting, roll the clay sheet and the texture plate together through the pasta machine. Peel the sheet and the plate apart.

7 shave raised area from pattern

Adhere the sheet of clay, pattern side up, to a smooth surface such as a ceramic tile or a piece of glass. Hold the clay blade so that it curves down slightly in the center, then carefully skim the blade along just the top of the clay sheet, shaving away the raised areas of the patterned surface.

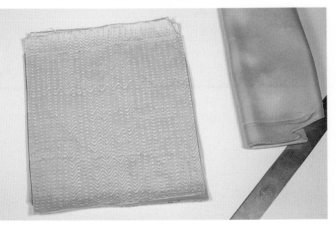

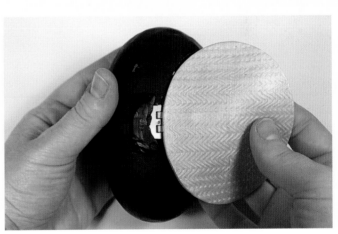

8 smooth patterned sheet

After all the raised texture has been shaved off, roll the clay sheet smooth. The sheet should maintain its patterned appearance, but its surface should feel smooth. Back the sheet with another thin sheet of pink clay to achieve a $1/8$" (3mm) thickness.

9 cut and place lid cover

Using an oval cutter slightly larger than that used to mark the lid, cut an oval piece from the patterned sheet. Press this piece on top of the base layer lid, lining it up evenly at the hinge and allowing it to extend out about $1/4$" (6mm) on all the other sides.

10 bake

Smooth out the oval piece with your fingers, working any air bubbles to the edges. Bake for 30 minutes.

11 mark vertical axis

With the pink lid attached, use a marker to draw a vertical axis on the egg, from the front, around the bottom, to the back.

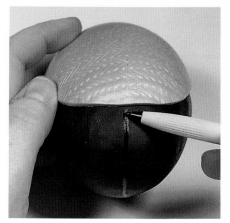

12 mark horizontal axis

Use a marker to draw a perpendicular axis from one end of the egg to the other.

13 create template

Gently fit a sheet of scrap clay over one quarter of the egg, trimming along the axis lines to create a template.

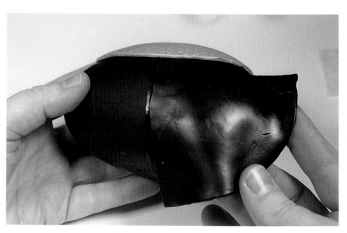

14 remove template

Carefully remove the template from the egg.

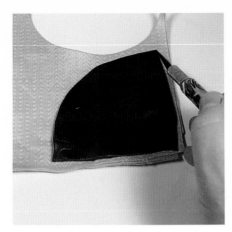

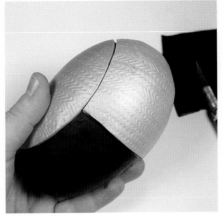

15 cut quarter sections from sheet
Use the template to cut four sections of the patterned sheet, one to cover each quarter of the egg. The pattern should run consistently from one piece to the other, so keep the orientation or "grain" of the pattern in mind as you lay out and cut the pieces.

16 add two quarters
Adhere one quarter section by pressing it firmly to the egg. Add another quarter section in the same manner, lining up its edges flush with the edges of the other pieces. Bake for 30 minutes.

17 add two more quarters
Add the two remaining quarters, butting the edges against the other sections. Don't worry about smoothing over the seams, as they will be covered later. Bake again for 30 minutes. When the clay is cool, sand the entire egg with 320-, 400-, 600- and 800-grit wet-dry sandpaper.

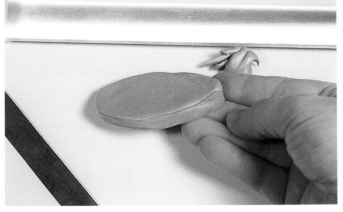

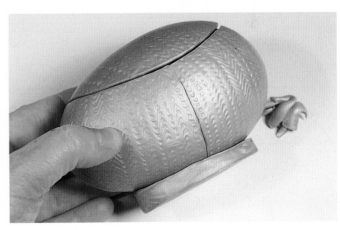

18 create base
Roll out an oval of pink clay for the base. Compensate for the curvature of the egg by creating a slope along the top of the base, with a thickness that runs from 3/8" (9mm) to 1/4" (6mm).

19 attach base
Press the egg onto the base to make it conform to the curve. Gently peel the base from the egg, add a bead of liquid polymer clay and reapply the base. Bake for 30 minutes.

20 create texture band mold

Condition the Sculpey SuperFlex Bake & Bend clay until it is very, very soft. Add some liquid polymer clay if necessary to achieve this soft consistency. Roll out a long snake of clay, then roll it through the pasta machine to a 1/8" (3mm) thickness. Lightly powder the strip with cornstarch to eliminate any tackiness. Place the textured bead on a double-pointed knitting needle. With even pressure, roll the bead along the length of the strip, impressing the pattern uniformly as the bead rolls along the clay surface.

21 finish band mold and bake

If the bead has an outside rim or edge, it will leave a deep line along the sides of the pattern. If the bead does not leave a deep line, add one by dragging the needle tool down each side of the pattern. This line defines the perimeter of the band. Finish by trimming off any excess clay, then bake the mold for 20 minutes.

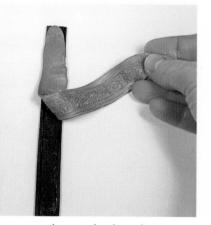

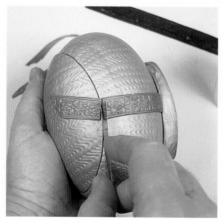

22 create decorative band

Roll a length of gold metallic clay to 1/16" (1.5mm) thickness. Powder the clay lightly with cornstarch to eliminate tackiness, then press it into the mold. Gently remove the clay from the mold and trim to the perimeter of the pattern. Repeat to create several decorative bands.

23 add decorative bands to egg

Apply a line of liquid polymer clay over each seam on the body of the egg. Place the decorative bands of textured gold clay over each seam, trimming wherever the band meets the edge of the lid.

24 add decorative band to lid

Apply a decorative band along the perimeter of the lid. Cut and join pieces of the band as necessary to achieve the curved shape. Open the hinged lid to make sure that the band does not impede the lid's mobility Trim away any clay if necessary.

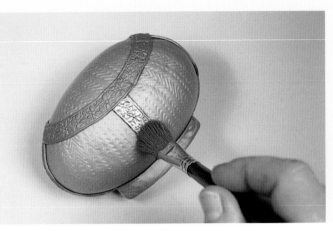

25 apply gold leaf to band

Cut lengths of gold leaf to the width of the decorative band. Press the leaf gently onto the bands until the leaf is released from the carrier sheet. Continue to apply the gold leaf until all the decorative bands are covered.

26 finish leafing and bake egg

Use the soft brush to gently tap the gold leaf into all the recesses of the pattern and smoothly adhere it. Bake for 30–40 minutes.

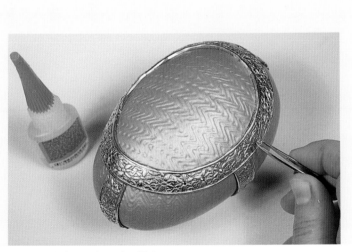

27 varnish and embellish

Apply two or three coats of water-based varnish over the entire egg, allowing a drying time of at least one hour between each coat. Using a pair of tweezers and cyanoacrylate glue, attach Austrian crystals to the gilded decorative bands.

Every Fabergé Imperial Egg had a surprise inside. Incorporate colors, textures and techniques from this project into other jewelry-making techniques from previous projects to make a necklace. In the spirit of Fabergé, hide the surprise necklace inside the box.

PROJECTS INSPIRED BY *fine art*

Whether or not you consider yourself a fine artist, your polymer clay work is probably influenced by fine art in one way or another. Perhaps you've developed your sense of design, your technique or your color palette from a particular art movement or a favorite artist. Or, maybe you've simply been inspired by the works that you've seen in a museum, a book or even a friend's studio. In this section, we'll embrace these influences by tapping into a variety of fine art sources.

The projects in this section focus on adapting polymer clay materials and techniques to simulate various effects associated with fine arts. With clay, you are able to achieve the brilliant translucent color of stained glass, the free-flowing brushwork of watercolor, the tightly controlled geometric pattern of a kaleidoscope and more. Because polymer clay is such a versatile medium, you'll be able to produce a wide range of masterpieces—the sign of true artistic genius!

raku
bathroom set

If you've ever seen a raku-fired ceramic piece, you may have observed an unusual metallic finish and a rough surface texture. These characteristics give many raku pieces their distinctive beauty. Luckily, you don't need to have a studio, a collection of glazes and a kiln to create raku-inspired polymer clay pieces. In this project, the reflective color effects of raku are simulated with the use of mica powder, and the irregular surface texture is imitated by adding a second layer of liquid clay. Begin the set by making the toothbrush holder, then complete it by creating a drinking glass and soap dispenser in the same fashion.

materials and tools

- 8 oz. (227g) black clay
- liquid polymer clay
- mica powders: blue, bronze, copper, gold, green, red and silver
- 2 matching 8–10 oz. (235–300ml) glasses
- lotion/soap dispenser bottle (glass or metal)
- water-based varnish
- acrylic rod or brayer
- craft knife
- dust mask
- oval cutter, approximately ¾" × 1" (2cm × 2.5cm)
- rubber stamp: unmounted border pattern, approximately 1" × 4" (2.5cm × 10cm)
- stiff-bristled brush
- 3 disposable cups

INSPIRATION: RAKU DISH

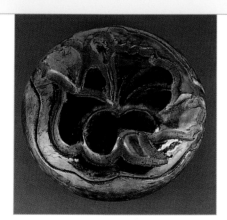

Raku is a ceramic technique in which fired pieces are removed from the kiln while still hot, then placed into a container of combustible materials such as wood chips or pine needles. The heat of the piece ignites the materials and the burning environment changes the glazes. The glaze undergoes deep, subtle color changes that can include very reflective metallic effects. This raku dish was made by artist Lillian Rubin.

1 apply clay trim

Roll out the black clay to a sheet ⅛" (3mm) thick. With a craft knife, cut a strip of clay to a width of ½" (13mm) and a length equal to the circumference of the glass rim. Gently press the strip around the interior of the rim. Butt the two ends together and smooth the seam. Trim the upper edge of the clay even with the top of the glass.

2 create lid

Cut a circle of black clay that is equal in size to the outer edge of the glass rim. With the oval cutter, cut out four evenly-spaced holes, radiating from the center of the circle. Squeeze a line of liquid polymer clay onto the top edge of the black clay rim inside the glass.

3 adhere lid and bake

Lay the lid over the top of the glass, pressing it into the liquid polymer clay. Bake. Cool.

4 add top to lid

Pop the lid off the glass and coat the top surface of the lid with liquid polymer clay. Cut a circle of black clay ⅛" (3mm) thick, with a diameter 1" (2.5cm) larger than the lid. Center the lid upside down on the clay circle. Using the existing ovals as a guide, cut ovals in the bottom sheet with a craft knife.

5 cover glass with clay

Replace the lid on the glass and smooth down the outer layer of clay over the edge of the rim. Cover the sides of the glass with a sheet of clay ⅛" (3mm) thick. Trim all the edges to meet, then smooth the side seam. Recut the lid line if the seam gets distorted or blended into the sides.

6 create pattern on surface

Mark a line around the clay-covered glass about 1" (2.5cm) from the top. Using the line as a guide, press the rubber stamp firmly around the glass, matching and repeating as necessary to make the pattern one complete ring around the surface of the glass.

7 apply mica powder

Select green, blue, copper and red mica powder. With your fingertips, generously apply the powder all over the surface, blending and overlapping colors. Bake. Cool.

8 apply metallic clay mixture

Pour a dime-sized pool of liquid polymer clay into each of the three mixing cups. In one cup mix silver mica powder, in another mix gold and in the last mix bronze. Using a stiff brush, pounce the silver, gold and bronze mixtures over the surface of the container, blending the colors.

9 finish surface

Continue to pounce until the surface is slightly pebbled. In addition to adding the slightly rough texture, this step mutes and blends the colors applied earlier. It also serves to hide all fingerprints, nicks and other imperfections in the clay surface. Bake. Finish with several coats of water-based varnish.

Complete the bathroom set by creating a drinking glass and soap dispenser. For the drinking glass, cover the matching glass, leaving at least 1" (2.5cm) of uncovered glass around the top edge. (Polymer clay is not appropriate for use with foods, so keep the clay from the area of the glass that will touch the mouth.) Cover the soap dispenser bottle to the threaded neck and trim any clay out of the way of the cap. Proceed with the application of the raku surface, as explained in steps 6–9.

stained glass
vase

If you're not yet convinced about the versatility of polymer clay, this project should sway your opinion. You'll be surprised how easy it is to imitate the look of stained glass using only liquid polymer clay and some ink. First, the lead cames of stained glass are simulated by drawing them directly onto the glass with black liquid polymer clay. Untinted liquid clay is then applied to the surface and ink is added, resulting in the characteristic marbled effect of stained glass. Once you gain experience transferring the design to the glass, you can create a signature piece with your own unique design.

materials and tools

- liquid polymer clay
- Piñata inks: Blanco Blanco, Sangria, Sapphire Blue and Sunbright Yellow
- oil paint: black
- smooth glass vase, approximately 10" (25cm) tall and 4" (10cm) diameter at the base
- craft knife
- cardstock (small piece) or index card
- graph paper
- heat gun
- needle tool or stir stick
- pen or marker
- small squeeze bottle with fine applicator tip

INSPIRATION: STAINED GLASS

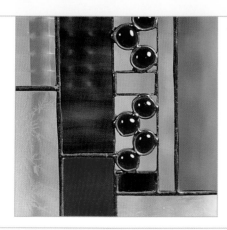

Stained glass reached a peak in popularity during the early twentieth century, when the Art Deco movement was highly influential. Today's stained glass artists, including Monicia Soder, the creator of the piece pictured at left, often draw upon the design principles of this movement.

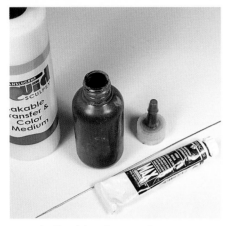

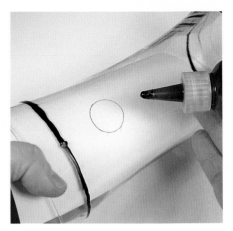

1 mix liquid polymer clay

In an empty squeeze bottle, mix about 1 oz. (30ml) of liquid polymer clay with ½ teaspoon (3ml) of black oil paint.

2 apply lines to glass

Use a small bottle with a fine applicator tip to apply a thin line of black liquid clay around the vase about 1" (2.5cm) from the top and bottom edges. Set the liquid clay with a heat gun or put the vase immediately into a pre-heated oven and bake for 10 minutes.

3 apply circles to glass

Draw a 1" (2.5cm) diameter circle on a piece of cardstock with a pen or marker. Place the cardstock inside the vase, holding the circle template up to the glass. Trace over the template onto the glass exterior with the black liquid polymer clay. Set each circle with the heat gun before drawing the next circle. Add about eight to ten circles at various points.

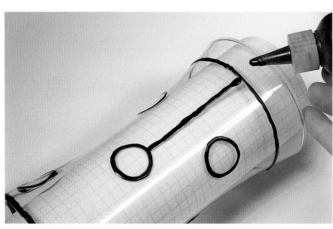

4 apply vertical and horizontal lines to glass

Roll up a sheet of graph paper and insert it into the vase so that it touches the interior surface and its edges are parallel to the top and bottom of the vase. Using the graph lines as guides, apply the black liquid polymer clay to the glass surface in vertical and horizontal lines originating at the circles. Continue until the surface is divided into a pleasing pattern. Bake the vase for 20 minutes to completely cure the liquid polymer clay.

5 clean up pattern

Using a craft knife equipped with a new, sharp blade, clean up the pattern by trimming off any accidental drips and straightening out all lines and corners.

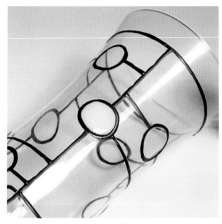

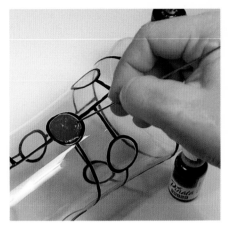

6 fill circle with liquid clay

Fill a circle with a smooth, even layer of untinted liquid polymer clay.

7 add ink to circle

Apply one drop of colored ink directly onto the wet liquid polymer clay and gently stir it in with a needle tool.

8 stir in color

Stir until the color is mostly blended but still slightly marbled, giving it the appearance of stained glass. Continue filling all the circles with different primary colors in the same manner, setting the liquid clay with a heat gun after each application.

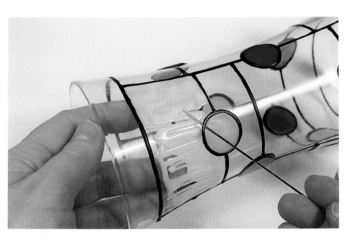

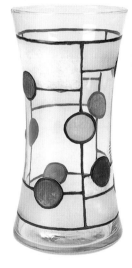

This Art Deco-inspired vase will dress up any room of the house.

9 fill in background

Fill some of the background spaces with untinted liquid polymer clay straight from the bottle. Smooth the liquid clay onto the surface. Fill other background spaces with liquid polymer clay, then stir in drops of white ink with a needle tool. Set the liquid clay with a heat gun after each application. Leave some background space as clear glass. Bake the vase one final time for 30 minutes to ensure the complete curing of all areas.

watercolor wash effect
frame

To imitate the watercolor medium, this project utilizes alcohol-based inks, specifically Piñata inks. You also may use several brands of art markers, such as Prismacolor, and some re-inking supplies for rubber stamping. Piñata inks contain a resin that helps harden and adhere the colorant to the clay. These resins are soluble in alcohol, but they harden quickly in the presence of water or when the alcohol evaporates. Other Piñata formulas, such as Claro Extender and Clean-up Solution, are also useful when working with inks on clay. With these products, it is possible to achieve a marbled, water-spotted or wash effect.

materials and tools

- 3–4 oz. (85–113g) white clay (or a pearl/white mixture in any proportion desired; see *Tip*, page 107)
- 2 oz. (57g) translucent clay, optional
- Piñata inks: several colors of your choice
- Piñata Claro Extender
- photograph frame (smooth metal; see *Tip* page 109)
- 1–2 sheets 23k gold leaf, optional
- 70% isopropyl (rubbing) alcohol
- water-based varnish
- acrylic rod or brayer
- clay blade
- craft knife
- metal ruler
- small and medium synthetic paintbrushes
- palette (glass or Plexiglas)
- pasta machine
- cup for alcohol
- index card
- waxed paper
- wet-dry sandpaper, 400-, 600- and 800-grit

INSPIRATION: ABSTRACT WATERCOLOR

Abstract watercolor painting is always fun. It provides the opportunity for you, the artist, to relax, let go of control and let the paint and water dictate the composition. It's a little like making a Rorschach ink blot—everyone is encouraged to see his or her own interpretation of what's in the picture.

1 paint the sheet

Roll out the white clay into a ⅛" (3mm) thick sheet, with the length about three-quarters the length of the frame and the width about four times the width of one frame side. Prepare a palette with two or three drops of each color ink, then thin the ink by adding two drops of Claro Extender to each color. Allow the palette to dry.

TIP

Piñata ink sets include two solutions called Claro Extender and Clean-up Solution. Claro Extender can be mixed with inks to increase transparency and decrease the saturation of a color. Claro will also redissolve resin that has previously hardened on a surface. This is useful to create marbled and water-spotted effects. Areas of color mixed with Claro will remain shiny. Clean-up Solution is concentrated alcohol with brush conditioners. It is useful as an extender and to redissolve resins that have hardened on the palette or paintbrush bristles. 70-percent rubbing alcohol may also be used with Piñata and other alcohol-soluble inks. Areas of color mixed with rubbing alcohol or Clean-up Solution will have a matte surface.

70-percent rubbing alcohol is diluted with water, which is important to know for two reasons: water is resisted by polymer clay and water causes the resin particles in the ink to "fall out of solution," or harden, more quickly. Thus, 70-percent alcohol is particularly useful for painting washes on larger spaces of clay because it will flow across the surface faster and will evaporate more slowly than ink diluted with pure alcohol. However, established lines or boundaries may bleed, or the rubbing alcohol may spread farther across the surface than desired. Also, when the resins harden due to the water, they may clog up the bristles of the brush or leave larger grains of color on the surface. I recommend that as you work on a design, especially in the landscape and floral projects, you use Claro Extender or Clean-up Solution for details and additional layers rather than rubbing alcohol.

2 apply wash to sheet

Select which color you would like to use as the base color on the frame. With a paintbrush, mix rubbing alcohol into this color of ink on the palette, creating enough wet color to make a wash over the entire sheet. Apply the ink wash to the clay surface, moving the brush side to side and down the sheet quickly. It may help to support the clay on an index card and raise it at an angle so that gravity may participate in moving the wash.

3 add color

After the wash has dried, add short, bold strokes of a second color. Continue to add a third and fourth color with brushstrokes or by tapping the brush against your finger to spatter color droplets onto the surface. Apply more color, mixing the primary color inks to produce other colors as desired.

4 add extender

When the sheet is well covered with a variety of colors, place a drop of Claro Extender directly onto the surface. Watch the extender mix the colors as it spreads. Continue adding drops of extender, spaced close together, until the surface is mottled and the mix of color is pleasing. Set the sheet aside to dry.

5 roll sheet and apply gold leaf

Roll 1 oz. (28g) of translucent clay into a sheet as thin as possible. Place a sheet of gold leaf onto the translucent clay and gently rub to transfer it from the carrier sheet to the clay.

TIP

When painting with ink on a polymer clay surface, you'll find that the characteristics of pearl clay are quite different from those of white clay. If pure pearl is used, the pearlescent quality of the clay will show through the translucent inks. Pure pearl, however, has a tendency to darken slightly when baked. The chalkiness of white clay absorbs the ink a bit more and has a matte effect on the ink. To have the best of both worlds, I mix the two kinds of clay together in approximately equal proportions.

TIP

Mokume gane refers to a Japanese technique of layering different colors of metal on a sheet. The sheet contour is altered, then the layers are exposed, creating a wood grain effect. In polymer clay, translucent clay and various foils and paints provide many variations on the mokume gane technique. This project calls for the use of a translucent mokume gane sheet. The mokume gane layer (shown in steps 5–12) is optional, but it is useful in sealing the color and allowing the frame to be sanded smooth before finishing.

6 make a mokume gane stack

Using a clay blade, cut and stack the translucent sheet with gold leaf into a loaf six to eight layers thick.

7 cut loaf

With the blade, cut the loaf in half horizontally, slicing diagonally through the stack from the upper-right corner to the lower-left corner.

8 consolidate block

Restack the two pieces, placing the bottom on the top. This should give you an uneven, irregular pattern in the layers. Roll the clay with an acrylic rod to consolidate the block.

9 create translucent sheet

Roll the other 1 oz. (28g) of translucent clay into a sheet as thin as possible. Holding the clay blade almost horizontal to the mokume gane block, shave thin pieces off the top and apply them to the clay sheet. Roll the slices flat onto the sheet with an acrylic rod.

10 roll out sheet

Use a pasta machine to roll the sheet as thin as possible. It may help to sandwich the clay within a folded piece of waxed paper. First, feed the fold into the machine, then insert the clay sheet, holding it vertically. Hold the clay away from the waxed paper so that they can pass through at independent rates, allowing the clay to stretch.

11 peel away waxed paper

Peel the waxed paper from both sides of the translucent clay sheet.

12 roll sheets together

Lay the translucent sheet over the painted clay sheet, gold side down. Taking care not to trap any air bubbles, roll the two sheets together through the pasta machine to a thickness of 3/32" (2mm).

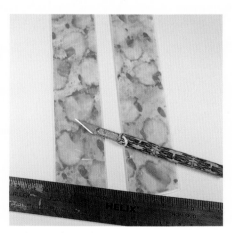

13 cut sheet into strips

Using a craft knife and a metal ruler, cut the sheet into strips at least ¼" (6mm) wider than the sides of the frame.

14 apply clay to frame

Apply the strips of clay to the surface of the frame, blending seams and pressing out any air bubbles.

15 trim excess clay

Turn the frame over and run a clay blade along the outside perimeter edges to trim any excess clay and create smooth edges.

16 bake and varnish frame

Use a craft knife to trim the inside edges smooth. Bake. Sand with 400-, 600- and 800-grit sandpaper, then finish with three coats of water-based varnish.

TIP

When choosing a frame to cover with polymer clay, it is best to use a smooth metal frame that has been cast or formed in one piece. Avoid the inexpensive brass frames that consist of metal strips with soldered joints, as these joints tend to expand and contract when heated and will cause cracking in the clay. Similar problems can occur with wooden frames. If you do use a wooden frame, bake it first to dry the wood; this will allow any shifting in the joints to occur before you cover it with clay.

Your favorite photograph is all you need to give this frame a finished look.

landscape
clock

I've always enjoyed making picturesque landscapes that depict a sunrise or sunset on the horizon. This project offers something more than the traditional landscape painting. The finished product is an original work of art *and* a clock. Polymer clay is an ideal surface for painting landscapes, as you can create wonderful effects with inks. The process of painting on clay is not very different from painting on paper; you begin your composition by applying the lighter colors first, then follow with darker colors and more detail. When your composition is complete, assemble the clock and enjoy!

materials and tools

- 3–4 oz. (85–113g) pearl/white clay mixture in any proportion desired (see *Tip*, page 107)
- 1 oz. (28g) black clay
- Piñata inks or Prismacolor markers: several colors of your choice
- Piñata Clean-up Solution
- clock kit for 3/8" (9mm) thick clock face
- 18k gold leafing pen
- 70% isopropyl (rubbing) alcohol
- acrylic rod or brayer
- circle cutter, 4 1/2" (11cm) diameter
- circle punch or brass tubing, 3/8" (9mm) diameter
- small and medium round synthetic paintbrushes
- palette (glass or Plexiglas)
- pasta machine
- cotton swabs
- cup for alcohol

INSPIRATION: LANDSCAPE PAINTING

What is your idea of the perfect landscape? Take advice from the late Bob Ross, the public television painting instructor, and make the landscape "your world" by including whatever inspires you: mountains or streams, the ocean or a prairie. I live in the midst of fertile farm ground, so my example is a field in early summer.

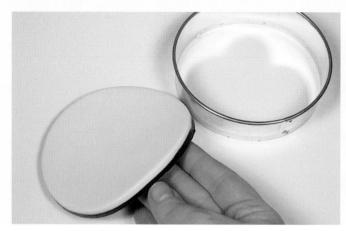

1 create clay disc

Mix the pearl and white clays until blended. With the pasta machine on its thickest setting, roll out a sheet of clay. Using the circle cutter, cut two circles from the sheet. Roll a sheet of black clay, again using the pasta machine at its thickest setting, and cut one circle with the circle cutter. Stack all the clay circles (white, white, black) and roll with the acrylic rod to consolidate. Recut the circle to achieve a smooth edge. The final disc of clay should be no more than ³⁄₈" (2mm) thick to fit the depth of the clock shaft.

2 prepare palette and begin landscape

Choose which color inks you would like to use, then prepare a palette by placing two or three drops of each color onto the glass and letting the ink dry. If desired, add alcohol or Clean-up Solution to the dry ink to dilute and lighten the colors. Scribble the Prismacolor marker on the glass, creating a pool of color to be picked up with the brush. Prepare wet color solutions to create a pale peachy yellow, light rose and sky blue. Working quickly with rubbing alcohol, paint the horizon and sky with the three colors and allow the inks to blend into each other.

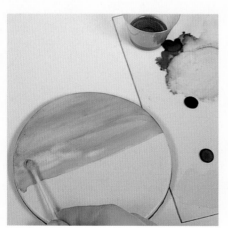

3 add clouds

If the lines of color appear too defined, repeat the wash again with the three colors to soften the blends. Using a clean cotton swab moistened with alcohol, erase areas for clouds.

4 paint sunlight and ground

Using slightly more intense colors, add the reflection of sunlight just along the lower edge of the clouds. Give the ground a base color wash of green.

5 add contours

Add some of the light and dark contours of the land with various shades of greens and browns.

6 add detail
Working with increasingly concentrated ink color and a drier brush, begin to add more detail to the landscape, such as these rows of plants.

7 paint background
Continue with another layer of darker detail and add some faint grays to the horizon to suggest trees or buildings in the distance.

8 mark center
Measure and mark the exact center of the clay circle. With a ⅜" (10mm) diameter brass tubing or a punch, make a hole in the center for the clock stem. Bake and cool.

9 finish edges and assemble clock
Paint the edge of the clock with a gold leafing pen. Assemble the clock according to the package instructions.

A one-of-a-kind timepiece like this makes a unique gift.

floral cover
memory book

When working with the watercolor medium, artists often apply the paint in layers, gradually adding more and more translucent colors. You can imitate this process by layering ink washes onto a clay sheet. In this project, the ink washes build upon one another, breathing life into magnolia blossoms. Not only will you be using polymer clay to create a beautiful cover for this memory book, you'll also be learning bookbinding techniques to assemble the pages. Using precut blank note cards for the book pages makes the process quick and easy.

materials and tools

- 2 oz. (57g) Ultramarine Blue clay
- 2 oz. (57g) black clay
- 2 oz. (57g) pearl/white clay mixture in any proportion desired (see *Tip* , page 107)
- liquid polymer clay
- Piñata inks or Prismacolor markers: black and dark blue, plus several colors of your choice
- 8 blank folded note cards plus 2 matching envelopes
- 1 sheet heavyweight paper: dark blue
- archival paper glue
- acrylic rod or brayer
- ball stylus
- craft knife
- metal ruler
- small and medium round synthetic paintbrushes
- palette (glass or Plexiglas)
- scissors
- texturing sheet or coarse sandpaper
- cotton swabs
- cup for alcohol

INSPIRATION: WATERCOLOR

This floral watercolor painting is one of my own creations. I learned watercolor techniques from an artist friend who specializes in realistic, close-up views of flowers. Her method is to apply several layers of watercolor, blending the edges of the color into the white paper for a soft look.

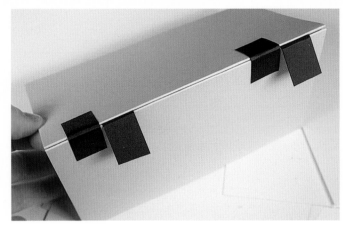

1 create hinges

Cut fourteen ¾" × 2" (2cm × 5cm) strips from the heavyweight paper, then fold each in half. Holding two note cards together in book fashion, place two of the strips over the folded edges of the cards like a hinge, one strip ¾" (2cm) from the bottom and the other 1½" (4cm) from the top. Glue the strips in place. Insert two more strips, placing one inside and the other outside the adhered strips. Slide one side of the strips between the two cards and glue. Leave the other side of the strip unattached, like a flap over the exterior of the card.

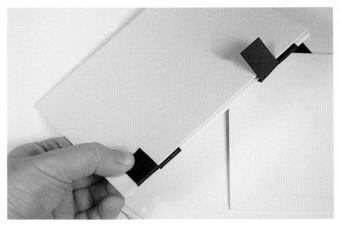

2 begin binding pages

Add a third folded note card, placing it under the flap of the unattached strips. Glue the strips over the folded edge of the card as a hinge.

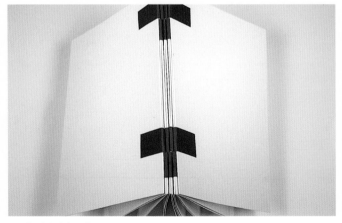

3 finish binding pages

Continue to add the remaining note cards, alternating the hinge strips around each adjacent pair of cards as in steps 1 and 2. Set the hinged note cards under a weight, such as a pile of books, to dry.

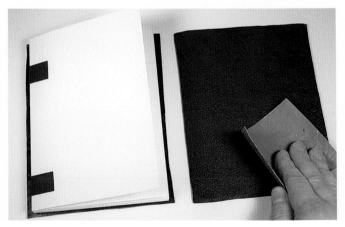

4 mix and roll out navy blue clay

Mix the Ultramarine Blue clay with the black clay to make an even navy blue color. Roll the clay into two ⅛" (3mm) thick sheets, approximately 5½" × 7½" (14cm × 19cm). Texture the surface with sandpaper or a texturing sheet. Bake.

5 trim sheets for book covers

Using a metal ruler and a craft knife, trim the edges of the covers so that both are straight and equal. Cutting is easier if the sheets are still slightly warm.

6 lay out design on white clay sheet

Roll the white clay mixture into a $\frac{1}{16}$" (1.5mm) thick sheet, approximately 4" × 5½" (10cm × 14cm). If you are using a reference photograph or picture for your design, lay it over the clay sheet and trace the major lines with a ball stylus, pressing just firmly enough to leave a discernible mark on the clay beneath. If you are not using a reference, lightly sketch the image directly onto the clay with the stylus.

7 prepare palette and begin painting

Prepare the palette with your selection of inks. Begin by applying color washes to the larger petal areas. Keep two brushes wet, one with color and the other with alcohol only. Make a stroke of color to define an edge, then pull the color into the petal shape with the alcohol-saturated brush.

8 continue adding washes

Continue applying ink in washes. Use clean cotton swabs to pick up any excess color which may pool or bead up on the clay surface. You can also wet the swab with clean alcohol to dab away any harsh lines or edges.

9 define flower petals

Continue to lay in the shapes and colors of each flower petal. To increase depth, paint additional layers of colors in more muted or contrasting tones.

10 apply base color

With a medium-value color, lay in the background base. Create a contour of the flowers by using the base color to outline the perimeter of each petal.

11 add dark blue and black ink to background

Use darker values to add detail to the flower until you are satisfied with the result. Apply a layer of thick, concentrated dark blue ink over the background. When dry, add a layer of black ink over the dark blue.

12 blend and soften background

Using a cotton swab saturated with alcohol, blend the background color and pull areas of color off the surface. Soften any brushstrokes, mix colors and lift away color to create a soft, out-of-focus effect.

13 adhere painting to cover

Coat the back of the painting with liquid polymer clay. Center the painting on one of the covers and gently smooth over the surface to adhere it. Bake the front cover again with the painting.

14 attach front cover to binding

Cut four ¾" × 5" (2cm × 13cm) strips of the dark blue paper. Place a strip below each hinge strip, then fold 1" (2.5cm) of the strip around the binding and glue it to the last card on the stack. Apply glue to the remaining length of the strips, then press the strips onto the inside surface of the front cover.

15 attach back cover to binding

With the two remaining strips of dark blue paper, repeat step 14 for the back cover.

16 finish inside of covers

Cut out the front side of an envelope. Trim one of the longer sides of the envelope front straight, then deckle or tear the three remaining sides. Glue this paper to the inside cover, covering the binding strips. Repeat for the second cover. Close the book and allow it to dry under a weight for several hours.

Use this memory book as a photo album, a scrapbook or a journal, letting the beauty of the covers reflect the beauty of what's inside.

kaleidoscope egg

If you haven't guessed by now, I was one of those weird kids in high school who really liked geometry class. Geometry underlies the basic process of caning, which is an important aspect of this project. As you create the kaleidoscope egg, you'll see that cane shapes are not always limited to circles and squares. When constructing your canes, make all the pieces an even width and all folds of the stripe as parallel as possible. Also, keep the angles precise at 45 and 90 degrees. This will ensure accurate mirroring throughout the length of the cane—and, after all, mirroring is fundamental to a kaleidoscope!

materials and tools

- 1–2 oz. (28–57g) scrap clay
- 1 oz. (28g) plus one walnut-sized ball of black clay
- 1 oz. (28g) cream or off-white clay
- 1 oz. (28g) dark red clay
- 1 oz. (28g) metallic gold clay
- metallic liquid acrylic paint: gold
- chicken egg
- acrylic rod or brayer
- brass tubing, ⅜" (9mm) diameter, 6"–8" (15cm–20cm) long
- circle cutters, 1¼"–2" (3cm–5cm) diameter
- clay blade
- muslin buffing wheel
- needle tools (sharp and thick)
- sponge
- wet-dry sandpaper, 400-, 600- and 800-grit

INSPIRATION: KALEIDOSCOPE

When you look inside a kaleidoscope, you see wonderful geometric, symmetrical designs that are generated by mirrors reflecting the changing shapes at one end of the tube. This mirroring effect is what inspired the eye-catching design of the kaleidoscope egg.

1 empty egg of contents

Using a sharp needle tool, pierce the smaller end of the egg and remove the egg contents as described in the *Tip* on page 88. Rinse the egg inside and out with warm water and allow it to dry for several days, or for 20–30 minutes in a warm (200°F/ 93°C) oven.

2 cover egg with clay

Roll the scrap clay into a sheet 1/16" (1.5mm) thick. With a clay blade, cut a strip about 2" (5cm) wide and approximately 1/2" (13mm) shorter than the widest circumference of the egg. Wrap the strip around the egg, stretching it to make the ends meet. Press the clay onto the shell, working the clay toward the open ends while gently working out any fullness. The ends of the egg will be exposed at this point.

3 cover the top and bottom

With a circle cutter, cut two circles from the clay to fit the top and bottom ends of the egg. Press one clay circle onto each end.

4 smooth and bake egg

Roll the brass tubing across the clay to close all the seams. Using the needle tool, pierce through the large hole in the shell to allow air to escape while baking. Bake and cool.

5 create Skinner blend

Create a Skinner blend with the dark red and gold clays. Roll the blend into a bull's-eye cane with the gold on the inside, as shown.

6 cut cane and stack sheets

Cut the bull's-eye cane into two equal lengths, about 2½" (6cm) each, then cut each lengthwise into random pieces. Roll out the black and white clay into separate sheets ¹⁄₁₆" (1.5mm) thick and 2½" (6cm) wide. Stack the black and white sheets, then roll out into a single sheet ¹⁄₁₆" (1.5mm) thick. Cut the length in half, stack again and roll out into a sheet ¹⁄₁₆" (1.5mm) thick. The edges of the stacked sheet should now be thinly striped black–white–black–white.

7 create clay cluster

Begin randomly arranging the red-and-gold pieces in a cluster, keeping the lengths of cane parallel to each other as you fold and wrap the black-and-white strip around and between them. Fold the black-and-white strip back on itself occasionally.

8 trim and shape clay

When all the red-and-gold pieces are incorporated, trim off the remaining black-and-white sheet with a clay blade. Shape the clay so that the color blend and the black-and-white stripe alternate around the edges. Do not try to use up all the black-and-white clay by wrapping it around the cluster, as this will create a closed shape.

9 compress and reduce cane

Compress the cane into a triangle and reduce the cane to at least double its length.

10 cut and reassemble cane

Use a clay blade to trim the uneven ends off the front and back of the cane, then cut the length into two equal pieces. Place the pieces together so that the ends mirror each other and form a square.

11 reduce and divide cane

Reduce the cane to 8"–10" (20cm–25cm) in length and approximately ½" (13mm) in width. Trim off the distorted ends and cut the length into four equal pieces.

12 form square cane

Arrange the four lengths so that the ends mirror each other and form a square. Compress and consolidate the cane, but do not reduce it further. At this point the cane should be approximately 2" (5cm) long and 1" (2.5cm) square in width. Let the cane rest for at least 30 minutes before moving on to the next step.

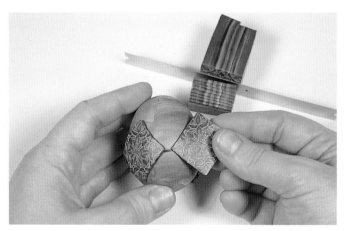

13 apply slices to circumference

Using a clay blade, cut ¹⁄₁₆" (1.5mm) slices from the end of the cane. Mark the widest part of the egg all around the circumference, then align the clay slices corner to corner along the marked circumference. Usually, four slices will fit around an egg, but some stretching or compressing may be necessary.

14 cover top and bottom

To cover the top of the egg, gently stretch and compress four slices into diamond shapes to fit into the pieces already placed along the circumference. Press the slices onto the egg, stretching or compressing until the edges barely meet and the top of the egg is covered. Repeat with four more diamonds on the bottom of the egg.

15 bake and polish egg

When the entire egg is covered, use an acrylic rod to smooth and blend the seams. Repierce the hole so that air can escape. Bake. Wet-sand the egg, starting with 400-grit sandpaper and progressing to 800-grit. Polish the egg on a muslin buffing wheel.

16 create display nest for egg

Form the remaining ball of black clay into a rough bowl shape. Press the bottom of the finished egg into the bowl to create a good fit. Make a nest texture around the outside of the bowl by using a needle tool to press and incise lines randomly on the surface. Bake and cool.

17 paint display nest

With your fingertip or a sponge, dab gold acrylic paint onto the raised surface of the nest, leaving the incised lines black. Allow the paint to dry.

Though decorative eggs are usually associated with the arrival of spring, you'll be proud to display this egg year-round!

All these patterns share the same geometric roots. Some appear very bold and graphic while others are fine and lacy. Each began as a blended cane, which was divided into random shapes and reassembled with a meandering stripe in the cane. Differences in the patterns result from the thickness of the stripe sheet, the number of layers of black and white in the stripe sheet and the scale to which the pattern was reduced.

resources

MANUFACTURERS

Eberhard Faber GmbH
Postfach 1220
02302 Neumarkt Germany
www.EberhardFaber.com
manufacturer of Fimo clays

Jacquard Products
Rupert, Gibbon & Spider, Inc.
P.O. Box 425
Healdsburg, CA 95448
(800) 442-0455
www.jacquardproducts.com
powders, paints, inks and dyes
manufacturer of Piñata products

Paper Parachute
P.O. Box 91385
Portland, OR 97291-0385
(503) 533-4513
www.paperparachute.com
rubber stamps

Penn State Industries
9900 Global Road
Philadelphia, PA 19155
(800) 377-7297
www.pennstateind.com
pen crafting kits

Poly-Tools, Inc.
Gale and Sue Lee
P.O. Box 10
Woodson, IL 62695
(800) 397-5201
www.poly-tools.com
tools

Polyform Products Co.
1901 Estes
Elk Grove Village, IL 60007

www.sculpey.com
manufacturer of Sculpey products

Puffinalia
Linda Geer
P.O. Box 46211
Seattle, WA 98146
www.puffinalia.com
Miracle Mold compound, supplies

Ready Stamps
10405 San Diego Mission Road, Suite 103
San Diego, CA 92108
(877) 267-4341
www.ucpsd.org/readystamps.htm
makes rubber stamps from your artwork

Tsukineko, Inc.
17640 NE 65th Street
Redmond, WA 98052
(800) 769-6633
www.tsukineko.com
manufacturer of Brilliance ink pads

Van Aken International
9157 Rochester Court
P.O. Box 1680
Rancho Cucamonga, CA 91729-1680
(909) 980-2001
www.katopolyclay.com
manufacturer of Kato Polyclay

PUBLICATIONS AND WEB SITES

Art Jewelry
Bead Style
Kalmbach Publishing
P.O. Box 1612
Waukesha, WI 53187-1612
www.beadandbutton.com

Belle Armoire
Somerset Studio
Stampington & Company
22992 Mill Creek, Suite B
Laguna Hills, CA 92653
(877) 782-6737 toll free
www.bellearmoire.com
www.somersetstudio.com

Expression Magazine
Publishers Development Corporation
12345 World Trade Drive
San Diego, CA 92128
(858) 605-0251
www.expressionartmagazine.com

National Polymer Clay Guild
www.npcg.org

PolymerCAFÉ
Mike and Joan Clipp
4640 Nantucket Drive SW
Lilburn, GA 30047
(678) 380-5783
www.polymercafe.com
print magazine devoted to clay

Polymer Clay Central
www.polymerclaycentral.com
clearinghouse for information and links related to polymer clay

Polymer Clay Polyzine
www.pcpolyzine.com
free online zine

index

The best in polymer clay projects and inspiration
is from North Light Books!

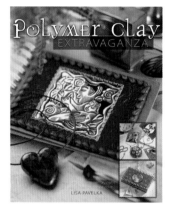

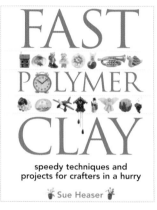

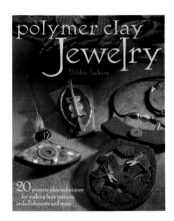

Filled with fresh designs, simple techniques and gorgeous colors, this exciting book combines two fun, easy-to-master crafts in one. You'll find guidelines for stamping images on all your clay creations, including jewelry, home décor and more, along with advice for experimenting with color and finish. The wide variety of projects guarantees spontaneous, delightful results.

ISBN 1-58180-155-6, paperback, 128 pages, #31904-K

Fast and fun, this book features 20 dazzling projects that combine easy polymer clay techniques with a variety of accessible mediums, including mosaic, wire stamping, foiling, millefiore, caning and metal embossing. Step-by-step instructions, full color photos and a section for beginners guarantees success. This unique guide also includes an inspiring idea gallery that encourages crafters to expand their creativity and develop original pieces of their own.

ISBN 1-58180-188-2, paperback, 128 pages, #31960-K

Sue Heaser shows you how to make over 50 stunning polymer clay creations, each in under an hour! This ingenious guide provides step-by-step instructions as well as tips and tricks for crafting stamped cards, a mosaic barrette, a faux jade pendant, miniature dollhouse accessories and more. Fit more creativity and crafting into your busy life with *Fast Polymer Clay*.

ISBN 1-58180-450-4, paperback, 112 pages, #32703-K

Create sophisticated and unique jewelry pieces with the popular and versatile medium of polymer clay. Inside professional teacher Debbie Jackson presents 20 step-by-step projects using a variety of creative jewelry-making techniques in four sections including additives and embellishments, textures, liquid polymer clay, and canes. This guide will provide you with the skills and creative spark you need to craft stunning pieces all your own.

ISBN 1-58180-513-6, paperback, 128 pages, #32873-K